Naturally Gourmet

Simple, plant-based recipes
that are healthy & delicious

KAREN HOUGHTON, RN, BSN

Hart Books

PO Box 2377, Fallbrook, CA 92088 · (800) 487-4278
www.NaturallyGourmet.com

Edited by Ken McFarland. Nutritional analysis by Eileen Kuninobu, RD. Designed by Mark Bond. Photography by Elena Gipson.
Additional Photography by Dan Houghton. Food stylist, Donna Hanson. Stock Photography by Jupiter Unlimited.
This book is not intended to diagnose or treat any medical conditions. Consult your physician before beginning any dietary plan.

TABLE OF CONTENTS

Foreword

Real living involves experiencing joy from all aspects of our lives. We have all heard the words of Socrates, "Thou shouldst eat to live; not live to eat." Many interpret this as a rejection of joyful eating. But I say that what we eat should greatly add to the joy of living. Sadly, many of us emphasize only short-term joy—that is, the pleasure of eating tasty food. I love tasty food, but there is an even greater joy—an enduring and long-lasting pleasure that comes only to those who eat abundantly of foods capable of healing and rejuvenating body, mind, and spirit.

Some believe that we must choose between the joys of food and the joys of optimal health. Karen Houghton has clearly shattered that myth. With this cookbook, she has shown that we can truly enjoy the pleasures of food. And we can do this while eating the very foods that are both the genesis of health and part of a divine solution against the majority of illnesses in this world.

Modern science now documents the presence of special properties in whole plant-based foods that can turn off disease-causing genes and turn on genes that promote health. But this transforming power of food is greatly enhanced when it is prepared to bring both long term and immediate joy.

Karen Houghton has done just that. With *Naturally Gourmet,*™ we can enjoy each day and anticipate the pleasure of each meal. Most important, *Naturally Gourmet* can help us anticipate many years of optimal health and the joys of a life well lived.

Wes Youngberg, DrPH, MPH, CNS
Clinical Preventionist & Nutrition Specialist
Youngberg Lifestyle Clinic
Temecula, California

Introduction

As a young girl, I grew up in Wisconsin—the dairy state. When I went away to a boarding school for high school, I decided to become vegetarian. I ate a fair amount of cheese and dairy products when I eliminated meat from my diet. When I attended college, I took the nursing program at Andrews University. I enjoyed my classes but especially enjoyed my public health classes and the cooking classes we did for the community. My professor, Charlotte Hamlin, inspired us to share simple health principles with people and teach them how good nutrition can help to prevent disease. Those principles always stayed with me.

My attention was again drawn to this when my father developed type 2 diabetes. My parents attended Weimar Institute, a lifestyle program in California that specializes in reversal of diabetes. It really helped my dad. When I saw the effect that exercise and a plant-based diet had on my father, my conviction grew even stronger.

I have worked in hospitals, home health, and long-term care facilities. I wanted to help people but felt limited in what I could do and say.

When we moved to California, I decided to hold a small vegetarian cooking class in my home. I talked with our pastor at the time, and he encouraged me to do it in our church fellowship hall. So I advertised in the local paper, and we had around 100 people in attendance. For fifteen years I've been doing cooking classes in our community and always have a great response. I did a series of cooking classes in Phoenix for the It Is Written Television Ministry, and we had more than 120 people in attendance. So many people have failing health, and they are looking for an answer outside of drugs that have side effects and often only treat their symptoms. There is a place for medication, but if you can avoid it, why not?

When I started teaching these classes, I decided it was time to eliminate dairy products from my diet, as well. I found I actually felt better. I was highly motivated to make tasty food, because we have two sons who weren't going to be too interested in this if it didn't taste good! One thing I found—when you come under conviction with something in your diet, don't expect everyone else to have that same conviction. Just make your food tasty enough that they'll want to eat it!

I've learned over and over to experiment until you get a good result. I've also tried different cookbooks and found some really good recipes, which are in this book because I've been using them for years in my classes and wanted to share them with you too. (They are used with permission, of course!) The recipes in this book are some of our family favorites. I hope you enjoy them and that they will be a blessing to you and your family.

Karen Houghton

Karen Houghton, RN, BSN

Dedication

In thinking of to whom I would want to dedicate this book, my mother, Florence Szmanda, is the first one who came to my mind. Mom always made very tasty and healthy food for us. She set a table that looked appealing, with lots of color, and now we know that the more color there is on your plate, the better off you are. (She made me eat my green beans!)

As a young girl, I was the first in my home to become a vegetarian. Mom was the next in line to follow suit. Then, when Dad developed type 2 diabetes and my parents went to Weimar, a lifestyle clinic in northern California. Mom learned a whole new way to cook. She faithfully made healthy and tasty food. She would tell me, "You just have to adapt, adapt, adapt"—when you find a recipe that has ingredients you can't use, get creative and adapt.

So I want to thank my Mom, for all she's taught me and the wonderful example she's been to me all my life.

Helpful Hints

A few things I want to share with you will benefit you tremendously. First is the value of adding seeds and nuts to your diet.

Studies done on women eating a handful of nuts (i.e.: walnuts, pecans, almonds) more than five times a week found they had less than half the risk of coronary artery disease, as compared with those who rarely or never eat nuts.[1] Eat your nuts raw without the added fat and salt.

Brazil nuts are high in selenium, which is linked to a reduced risk for cancer and atherosclerosis. Eat at least three unsalted Brazil nuts a day. Just one provides 160 percent of our RDA for selenium.[2]

At all costs, avoid trans fats. Become a label reader. If something you pick off the shelf at the grocery store says "partially hydrogenated oils" or "hydrogenated vegetable oils," put it back. Don't bring it home. It clogs your arteries. You find these fats in things like peanut butter, pancake mix, crackers, cookies, etc. Also, check the labels in your pantry—you might be surprised. Trans fats contribute to type 2 diabetes. The Harvard School of Public Health found that every 2 percent increase in the number of calories from trans fat raises the risk of type 2 diabetes by 39 percent.[3] And the Rush Institute for Healthy Aging in Chicago found that eating significant amounts of "partially hydrogenated" vegetable oil increased one's risk of Alzheimer's disease by nearly two and one half times![4]

So what's so great about seeds? That's where lots of minerals are found—calcium, copper, iron, magnesium, selenium, and zinc, as well as vitamin E. Try different seeds on each given day—sunflower seeds, sesame seeds, pumpkin seeds—and make sure you get in flax seeds and chia seeds.

Flax seeds actually reduce inflammation in the body and help prevent blood clots. They lower cholesterol and triglycerides, help protect against deadly heart rhythms, and help arteries open wider.[5] That's a lot of benefits from those tiny seeds. You can't benefit from them, though, until you grind them up in a nut or seed grinder. Once they are ground, store them in the refrigerator for up to twenty-four hours. After twenty-four hours, they lose their nutritive value. So buy your seeds whole, not ground, and grind them yourself.

Chia seeds are also high in omega 3 fats and they don't have to be ground. Great for travel.

Remember each day—a handful of nuts, 2 - 3 Tbs of seeds, at least 8 glasses of water, 40 grams of fiber, 45 - 60 minutes of exercise, an attitude of gratitude and time in God's Word. You are well on your way to improved health. God bless you as you make strides to live a healthy and fulfilled life.

1. F. B. Hu. "Frequent Nut Consumption and Risk of Coronary Heart Disease in Women: Prospective Cohort Study," *BMJ*, 1998, 317:1314-1345.
2. *Food Science and Technology*, volume 42, issue 10, December 2009.
3. J. Salmeron. "Dietary Fat Intake and Risk of Type 2 Diabetes in Women," *American Journal of Clinical Nutrition*, 2001, 73:1019-1026.
4. M. C. Morris. "Dietary Fats and the Risk of Incident Alzheimer Disease," *Archives of Neurology*, February 2003, 60 (2): 194-200.
5. *Dr. Arnott's 24 Realistic Ways to Improve Your Health*. p. 33.

Fiber in Foods

These pages are intended to help you keep track of how much fiber you are getting in a day. I've made a little slogan to help you remember how important it is:

"If you want to lose weight and keep disease away, eat 40 grams of fiber, every single day!"

Remember, fiber is found only in plant foods—there is no fiber in meat or dairy products.

Try keeping track of just how much you are getting in a day. The average American gets about 10 grams a day—a far cry from where we should be.

This information will help you on your journey to better health.

The recipes in this book have the dietary fiber listed for each recipe. These fruits, vegetables, grains, beans, and nuts can supplement your recipe to bring your total up.

Fiber Content in Fruit

Avocado—1 med.	12 gm	Mango—1 C	3.0 gm
Papaya—1 med.	5.5 gm	Guava—1	3.0 gm
Pear—1 med.	5.5 gm	Kiwi—1	2.5 gm
Dried figs—5	5.0 gm	Cranberries—½ C	2.0 gm
Apple—1 med.	4.4 gm	Pineapple—1 C	2.0 gm
Raspberries—½ C	4.0 gm	Grapefruit—½	1.7 gm
Blackberries—½ C	4.0 gm	Peach—1 med.	1.6 gm
Shredded coconut—½ C	4.0 gm	Apricots—2	1.5 gm
Blueberries—1 C	3.6 gm	Date—1	1.5 gm
Prunes—3	3.5 gm	Cantaloupe—¼ sm.	1.4 gm
Strawberries—1 C	3.3 gm	Raisins—2 Tbs	1.3 gm
Orange—1	3.1 gm	Grapes—12	0.5 gm
Banana—1	3.1 gm		

Fiber Content in Vegetables*

Peas	4.4 gm
Brussels sprouts	4.0 gm
Corn	4.0 gm
Baked potato with skin—1 med.	4.0 gm
Sweet potatos/Yams	3.8 gm
Winter squash	3.0 gm
Hominy	3.0 gm
Carrots—1 raw or ½ C cooked	2.3 gm
Broccoli	2.5 gm
Spinach, collard greens	2.1 gm
Romaine lettuce—2 C	2.0 gm
Asparagus	2.0 gm
Green beans	2.0 gm
Okra or turnips	2.0 gm
Beets	1.6 gm
Bean sprouts	1.5 gm
Kale	1.3 gm
Zucchini, cooked & sliced	1.2 gm
Mushrooms, raw	1.0 gm
Summer squash	1.0 gm
Tomato—1 med.	1.5 gm
Lettuce	0.5 gm
Cauliflower, raw—1 floret	0.3 gm

Fiber Content in Legumes*

Navy beans	9.5 gm
Pinto beans	9.4 gm
Black beans	7.5 gm
Lentils, pinto beans	7.0 gm
Large lima beans	6.6 gm
Garbonzos	6.2 gm
Kidney beans	5.5 gm
Split peas, cooked	4.4 gm

Fiber Content in Nuts & Grains

Pearled barley—1 C, cooked	6.0 gm
Oats—1 C, cooked	4.0 gm
Brown rice—1 C, cooked	3.5 gm
Nuts/seeds—¼ C	3.0 gm
Ground flax seeds—1 Tbs	2.5 gm
Chia seeds—1 Tbs	2.5 gm
Peanut butter—1 Tbs	1.0 gm
Almond butter—1 Tbs	1.0 gm
Wheat germ—1 Tbs	1.0 gm

*(1/2 C cooked, unless noted)

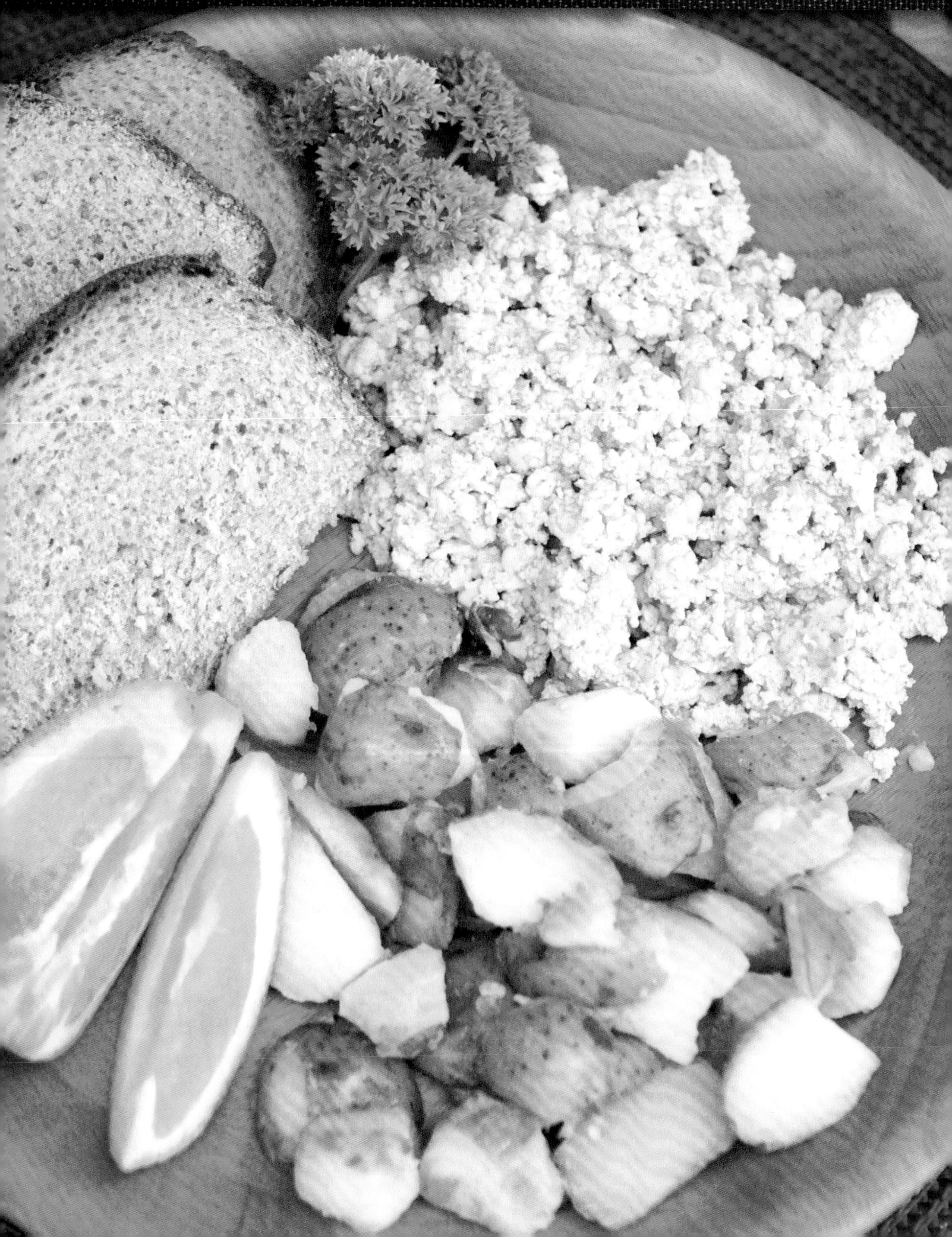

Scrambled Tofu

1 lb tofu, firm

½ tsp salt or less

¼ tsp garlic powder

1 Tbs nutritional yeast flakes

1 clove minced garlic

2 tsp McKay's or Bill's Best Chicken Style Seasoning

½ tsp turmeric powder

½ tsp onion powder

½ C chopped onions

¼ tsp celery salt

Crumble or mash tofu and set aside to drain. In a large skillet, sauté onions in Pam-sprayed pan until soft. Add spices to mashed tofu and then add tofu to onions in the skillet. Turn tofu mixture, as needed, over medium heat until liquid evaporates. (Suggested additional seasonings: cumin, paprika, hickory seasoning, curry powder.)

Variations: You may add, in addition to onions, chopped green peppers, sliced mushrooms, black olives, etc. Scrambled tofu can be made into mock egg salad by deleting mushrooms and adding Vegenaise to moisten, and chopped pickles. If you prefer, you can bake the scrambled tofu in the oven for an hour at 350° instead of cooking in the skillet. (Bake until the liquid is evaporated.)

Nutrition Facts (1 serving = 1/5 recipe)

Calories 146, Fat 8 g, Saturated 1 g, Trans fat 0 g, Cholesterol 0 mg, Sodium 393 mg, Carbohydrate 7 g, Dietary fiber 3 g, Protein 16 g, Vitamin A 3%, Vitamin C 3%, Calcium 62%, Iron 15%

(Tofu has no fiber in it, so adding veggies to it will give it some fiber. It also has no cholesterol, which is a big bonus!)

Biscuits & Gravy

Biscuits

3 C unbleached flour

1 C whole wheat flour

5 tsp Rumford baking powder

2 tsp salt

½ C extra-light olive oil

1 ¾ C water

Mix dry ingredients. Mix oil and water and add to dry ingredients. Roll the dough out on a floured board and use a biscuit cutter to make biscuits. Put the biscuits on an oiled cookie sheet. Bake at 400° for 20 minutes or until the top of the biscuits are lightly browned. Makes about 20 biscuits.

Gravy

3 C water

½ C washed raw cashews

½ C unbleached flour

Blend in blender until smooth.

Pour cashew gravy into a kettle. Cook over medium temperature until gravy thickens. Stir with wire whisk. Season with Lawry's seasoned salt or Mrs. Dash, if on a low-sodium diet. You can add Morningstar Farms Breakfast Patties, crumbled, Links, or chopped Stripples to the gravy, if desired. This gravy makes enough for 3-4 people.

(Hint: If you want to increase the fiber, use 2 C whole wheat pastry flour and 2 C unbleached flour. Add plenty of fresh fruit for an extra boost.)

Biscuit Nutrition Facts (1 biscuit)
Calories 81, Fat 6 g, Saturated fat 1 g, Trans fat 0 g, Cholesterol 0 mg Sodium 454 mg, Carbohydrate 7 g, Dietary Fiber 1 g, Protein 1 g, Vitamin A 0%, Vitamin C 0%, Calcium 16%, Iron 3%

Gravy Nutrition Facts (1 serving = ¼ recipe)
Calories 141, Fat 7 g, Saturated fat 2 g, Trans fat 0 g, Cholesterol 0 mg, Sodium 6 mg, Carbohydrate 17 g, Dietary Fiber 1 g, Protein 4 g, Vitamin A 0%, Vitamin C 0%, Calcium 2%. Iron 10%

Brown Rice Pudding

2 C cooked brown rice

½ C chopped dates

½ C chopped raisins

½ C raw cashews

¼ tsp cinnamon

¼ C dried, fresh or frozen chopped pineapple

2/3 C or enough water to blend

1 Tbs honey or maple syrup

Preheat oven to 350°. Mix rice, dates, raisins, cinnamon, and pineapple in a bowl. Blend cashews, water, and honey until creamy. Add blended ingredients to rice mixture and combine well. Place in a well-oiled casserole dish and bake for 30 minutes. Serve warm with soymilk or pear cream (see p. 21).

Recipe adapted from *The Best of Silver Hills Cookbook*.

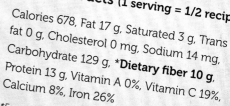

Nutrition Facts (1 serving = 1/2 recipe)

Calories 678, Fat 17 g, Saturated 3 g, Trans fat 0 g, Cholesterol 0 mg, Sodium 14 mg, Carbohydrate 129 g, ***Dietary fiber 10 g,** Protein 13 g, Vitamin A 0%, Vitamin C 19%, Calcium 8%, Iron 26%

For recipes highest in dietary fiber, the fiber content will appear in **bold in Nutrition Facts boxes.*

Granola

7 C quick oats

1 Tbs stevia

1 C unsweetened coconut

1 C slivered almonds

1 C wheat germ

½ C chopped walnuts

¼ C sunflower seeds

1 ½ tsp vanilla

1 tsp salt

½ C extra-light olive oil

½ C water

Mix the dry ingredients. Combine the liquids and add them to the oat mixture. Spread a thin layer on two large cookie sheets.

Bake at 225° for 1 to 1 ½ hours until crisp. Stir every ½ hour. You can bake this overnight with the oven temperature at 200°. Top with fresh fruit, ground flax seeds, and soy or almond milk. Makes about 12 servings.

(Hint: If you don't have access to stevia, you can use ½ C organic sugar or cook about 2C of dates in some water, blend them up, and add to the granola for sweetener.)

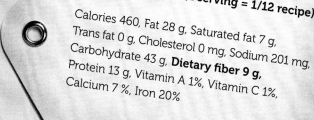

Nutrition Facts (1 serving = 1/12 recipe)

Calories 460, Fat 28 g, Saturated fat 7 g, Trans fat 0 g, Cholesterol 0 mg, Sodium 201 mg, Carbohydrate 43 g, **Dietary fiber 9 g,** Protein 13 g, Vitamin A 1%, Vitamin C 1%, Calcium 7 %, Iron 20%

Almond Milk

4 dates

4 C water

2/3 C almonds

½-1 tsp vanilla

Pinch of salt

If your blender is not a Vitamix or Blendtec, you will need to boil the dates in a little water before blending them. After blending all the ingredients until smooth, strain the milk with a large strainer (or milk-straining bag, widely available online) and pour in the pitcher. Shake well before pouring on your cereal.

Nutrition Facts (1 serving = 1/5 recipe)

Calories 132, Fat 10 g, Saturated Fat 1 g, Trans Fat 0 g, Cholesterol 0 mg, Sodium 40 mg, Carbohydrate 9 g, Dietary Fiber 3 g, Protein 4 g, Vitamin A 0%, Vitamin C 1%, Calcium 6%, Iron 5%

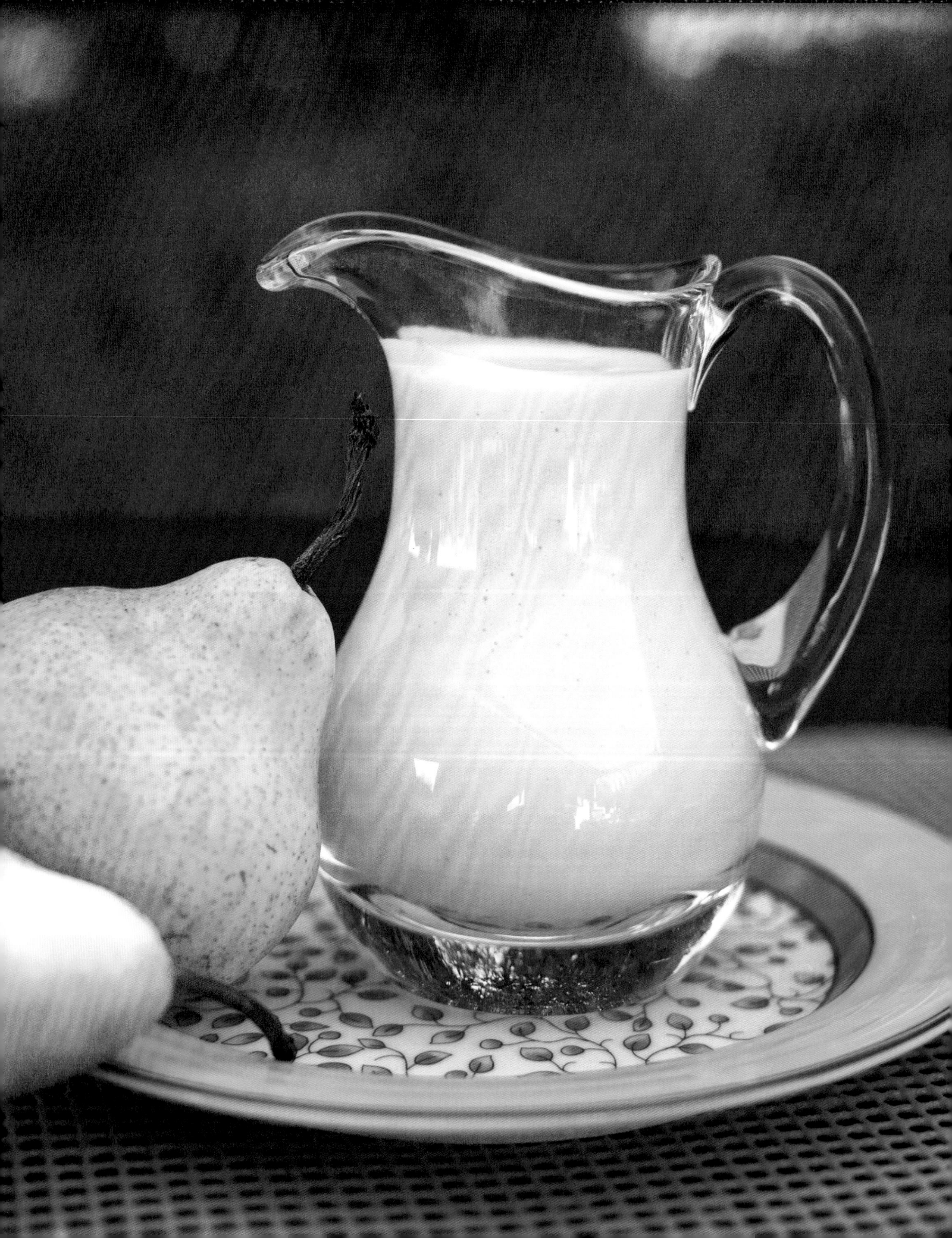

Pear Cream

½ C raw cashews

¼ tsp salt

1 tsp honey

1 qt canned pears in fruit juice

1 C fruit juice from canned pears or water

Place nuts in the blender. Add pear juice and blend until smooth. Add remaining ingredients until the milk is smooth and thick. Chill. Great on fruit salad, Brown Rice Pudding (p. 15), or other hot cereals.

Recipe from the
Best of Silver Hills Cookbook

Nutrition Facts (1 serving = 1/4 recipe)

Calories 214, Fat 7 g, Saturated fat 2 g, Trans fat 0 g, Cholesterol 0 mg, Sodium 155 mg, Carbohydrate 39 g, Dietary Fiber 4 g, Protein 3 g, Vitamin A 0%, Vitamin C 6%, Calcium 5%, Iron 10%

Crock-Pot Cereal

1 C steel cut oats

3 C water or more

Pinch of salt to taste (optional)

Put ingredients in the crock-pot and put on low setting at night—when you get up in the morning, breakfast is ready! Then top with your ground flax seeds, chia seeds, chopped nuts, and fresh fruit. You can pack a lot of fiber into this breakfast. Serves 2 - 3.

Nutrition Facts (1 serving = 1/3 recipe)

Calories 200, Fat 3 g, Saturated fat 1 g, Trans fat 0 g, Cholesterol 0 mg, Sodium 9 mg, Carbohydrate 36 g, Dietary fiber 5 g, Sugars 7 g, Protein 7 g, Vitamin A 0%, Vitamin C 0%, Calcium 1%, Iron 13%

WORLD'S COLUMBIAN EXHIBITION
CHICAGO, 1893
JOHN MCCANN'S
STEEL CUT
IRISH OATMEAL
CERTIFICATE OF AWARD
UNIFORMITY OF GRANULATION.
Approved N.B. CRITCHFIELD.
President of Departmental Committee.
Signed CHAS. KEITH.
Individual Judge
Dated 28th June 1894.
Approved JOHN BOYD THACHER.
Chairman Executive Committee of Awards
NET WT. 28 OZ (1LB 12 OZ) 793g

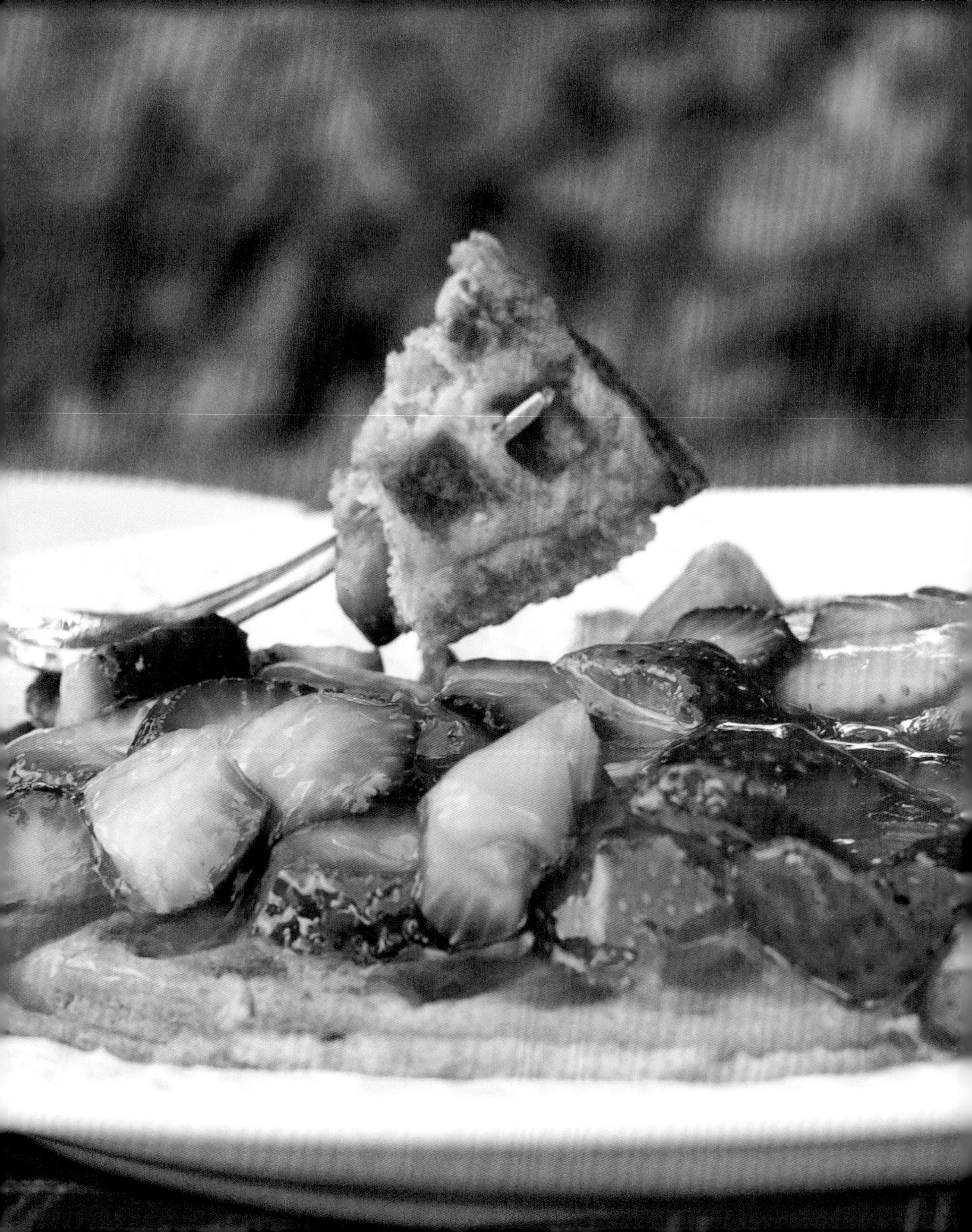

Waffles

1 C whole wheat pastry flour

½ C unbleached flour

½ C rolled oats

1 ½ tsp Rumford baking powder

2 ½ C organic soymilk

2 Tbs extra light olive oil

¼ C pure maple syrup

1 tsp vanilla

1 tsp cinnamon (optional)

Blend all ingredients in a blender. Let stand for a few minutes to thicken. Blend briefly before pouring onto a hot waffle iron. Spray waffle iron with olive oil spray before pouring waffle batter onto waffle iron. Cook for 10-12 minutes or until nicely browned. Makes 3 waffle squares of 4— or 12 waffles.

Hint: You can add 1 Tbs of ground flax seed to add another 2.5 gm of fiber to the total. Just blend with the other ingredients. You can sprinkle more on top of the nut butter you spread on the waffle and then top with fruit. (See pg. 35 for fruit topping recipe.)

Nutrition Facts (1 serving = 1 waffle)

Calories 129, Fat 4 g, Saturated 1 g, Polyunsaturated 1 g, Monounsaturated 2 g, Trans fat 0 g, Cholesterol 0 mg, Sodium 139 mg, Carbohydrate 21 g, Dietary fiber 2 g, Protein 5 g, Vitamin A 3%, Vitamin C 0%, Calcium 11%, Iron 8 %

Banana Waffles

1 C whole wheat pastry flour

½ C unbleached flour

½ C rolled oats

1 ½ tsp Rumford baking powder

2 ½ C organic soymilk

2 Tbs extra light olive oil

¼ C pure maple syrup

1 - 1 ½ tsp banana flavoring

½ - 1 banana

1 tsp cinnamon (optional)

Blend all ingredients in a blender. Let stand for a few minutes to thicken. Blend briefly before pouring onto a hot waffle iron. Spray waffle iron with olive oil spray before pouring waffle batter onto waffle iron. Cook for 10-12 minutes or until nicely browned. Top waffle with almond butter, ground flax seed, sliced bananas, and chopped walnuts; then drizzle pure maple syrup on top. Makes 3 waffle squares of 4—or 12 waffles.

Nutrition Facts (1 waffle)

Calories 129, Fat 4 g, Saturated 1 g, Polyunsaturated 1 g, Monounsaturated 2 g, Trans fat 0 g, Cholesterol 0 mg, Sodium 139 mg, Carbohydrate 21 g, Dietary fiber 2 g, Protein 5 g, Vitamin A 3%, Vitamin C 0%, Calcium 11%, Iron 8 %

Strawberry-Raspberry Sauce

10 pitted dates

1 - 1 ¼ C pineapple or pineapple-orange juice

1 Tbs organic cornstarch

2 C sliced strawberries

2 C raspberries

Cook dates in a little water, unless you have a Vitamix or Blendtec blender. Blend dates, juice, and cornstarch in blender. Pour mixture into a kettle and bring to a boil. When thickened, stir in 2 C sliced strawberries and 2 C raspberries. You can mash them with a potato masher.

Put this topping on waffles, pancakes, or peanut-buttered toast. Topping is also great on cooked cereal or granola. You can add more fresh strawberries and raspberries as a topping. Serves 4.

Hint: I add some strawberries to the blender, as well, making the sauce red and creamy.

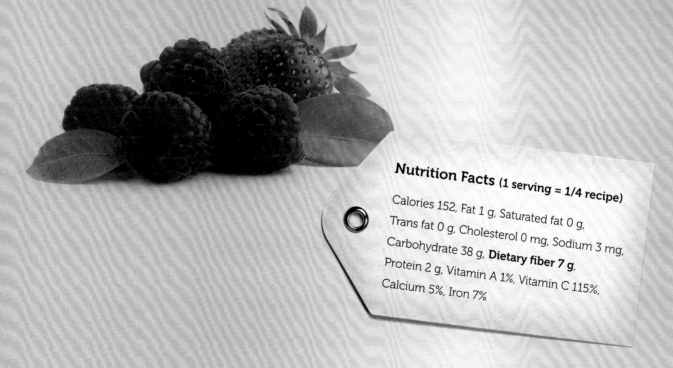

Nutrition Facts (1 serving = 1/4 recipe)

Calories 152, Fat 1 g, Saturated fat 0 g, Trans fat 0 g, Cholesterol 0 mg, Sodium 3 mg, Carbohydrate 38 g, **Dietary fiber 7 g**, Protein 2 g, Vitamin A 1%, Vitamin C 115%, Calcium 5%, Iron 7%

Cornmeal Grits

1 C whole grain organic cornmeal

3 C water or more

½ tsp salt

Bring the water to a boil and add the salt and grits. Continue to stir and reduce heat to low. Cook for about 30 minutes. Another option is to put all the ingredients in a crock-pot and cook on low overnight. Adding pumpkin seeds gives it a nice crunch–and drizzle some honey or pure maple syrup on top. Yummy! Serves 2-3.

Nutrition Facts (1 serving = 1/3 recipe)

Calories 147, Total fat 1 g, Saturated fat 0 g, Trans fat 0 g, Cholesterol 0 mg, Sodium 409 mg, Carbohydrate 31 g, Dietary fiber 3 g, Sugars 0 g, Protein 3 g, Vitamin A 2%, Vitamin C 0%, Calcium 1%, Iron 8%

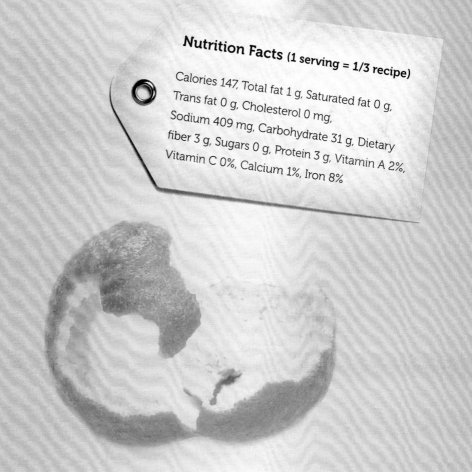

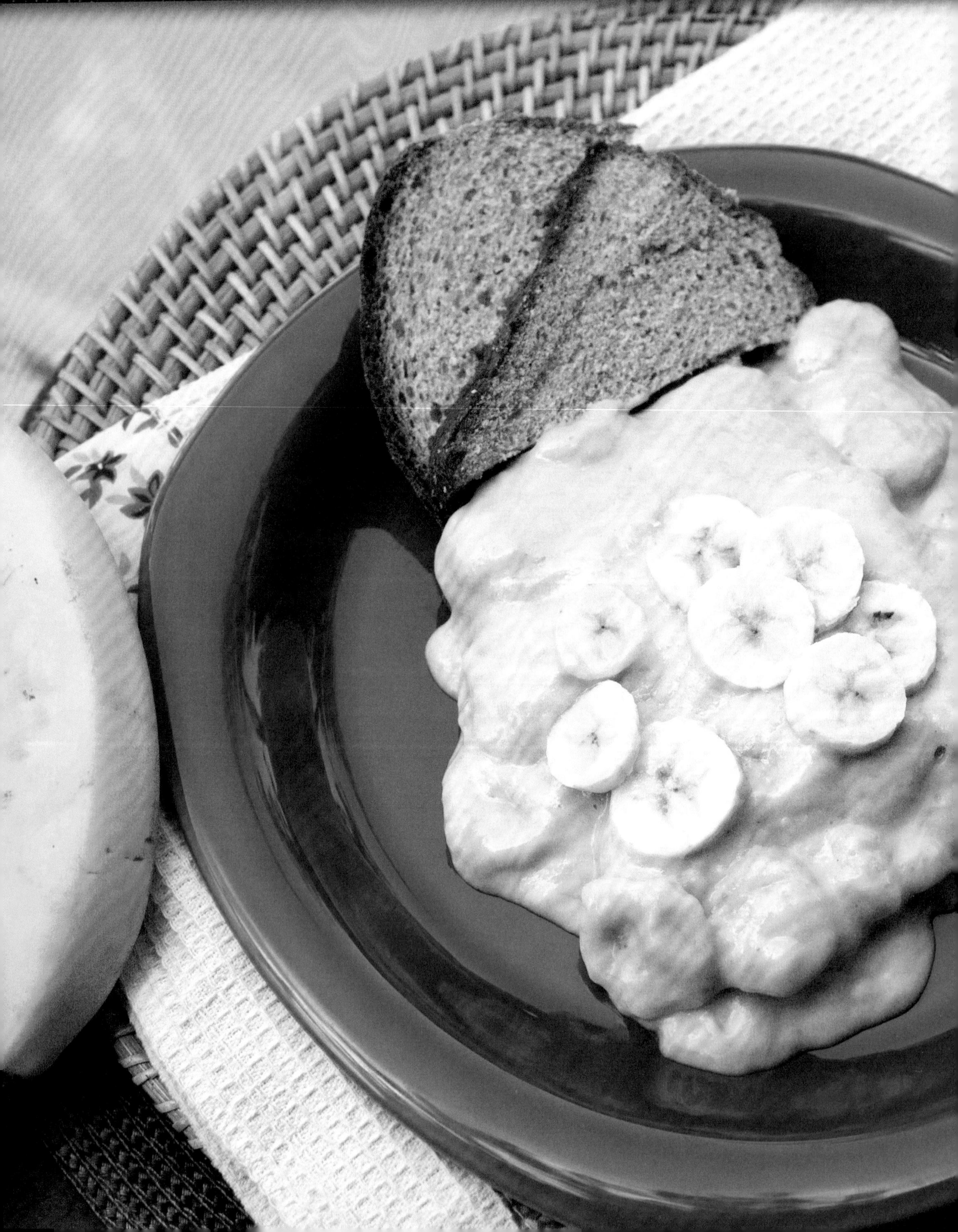

Banana Creme

3 C water

½ C washed raw cashews

½ C unbleached flour

1 tsp vanilla

1/3 C organic sugar or sweetener of your choice to taste

2 - 3 sliced bananas

Blend water and cashews in blender until smooth. Add flour and blend again. Pour cashew milk into kettle and cook until thickened. Add vanilla, sucanat, brown sugar, or maple syrup to taste and sliced bananas. Pour the banana creme over peanut-buttered whole grain toast. Serves 4.

(Hint: If you put this on whole grain toast, you can add 4 or more grams of fiber to your total grams)

Nutrition Facts (1 serving = 1/4 of creme recipe on 1 slice whole wheat toast)

Calories 340, Fat 8 g, Saturated fat 2 g, Trans fat 0 g, Cholesterol 0 mg, Sodium 140 mg, Potassium 354 mg, Carbohydrate 62 g, Dietary fiber 5 g, Sugars 26 g, Protein 9 g, Vitamin A 1%, Vitamin C 9 %, Calcium 6%, Iron 14%

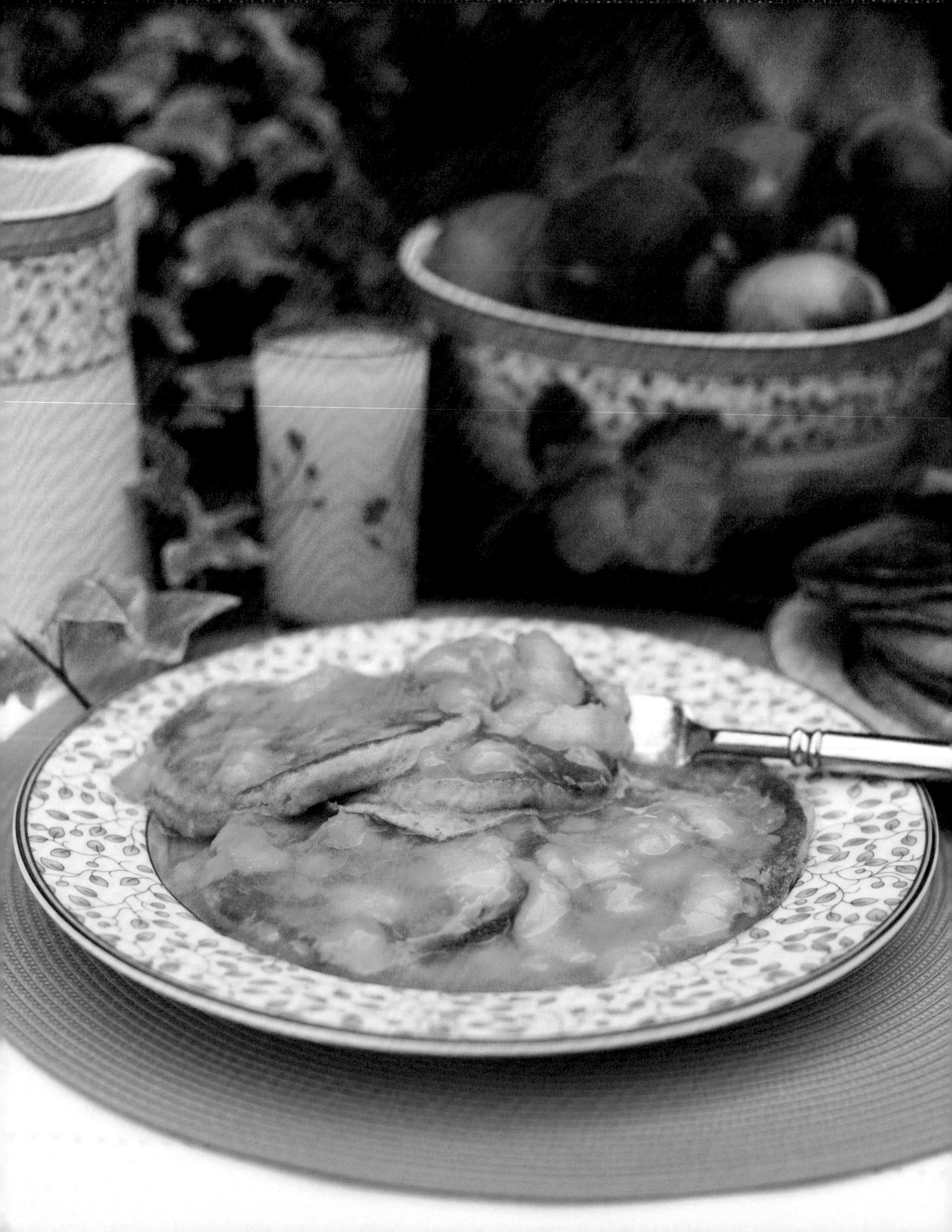

Blueberry Pancakes

Pancakes

¾ C whole wheat flour

½ C unbleached flour

1 ¼ C organic soymilk

1 ½ tsp vanilla

½ - 1 C blueberries

2 tsp baking powder

½ tsp cinnamon

1 Tbs light olive oil

1 Tbs honey

Mix the dry ingredients. Mix the liquid ingredients. Add the liquid to the dry ingredients and then add the blueberries.

Pour about ¼ C of batter onto a hot, oiled, non-stick skillet.
Turn the pancakes when they begin to bubble. Makes 15 pancakes.

Fruit Topping

1 quart frozen peaches defrosted or 5 - 6 fresh peaches (or fruit of your choice)

1 can frozen 100% apple juice or white grape juice

1 can of water   4 Tbs organic cornstarch

Mix the frozen juice, water, and cornstarch and bring to a slow boil until it thickens.
Then add the defrosted or fresh peaches.

Hint: This topping is wonderful with all kinds of different fruits. Blackberries have 8 g of fiber in one cup. I have used blueberries, peaches, strawberries, mixed berries, or mangos, and they all are tasty on top of pancakes or toast.

Pancake Nutrition Facts (1 pancake)

Calories 99, Fat 3 g, Saturated fat 0, Polyunsaturated 1g, Monounsaturated 2g, Trans fat 0, Cholesterol 0 mg, Sodium 136 mg, Potassium 89 mg, Carbohydrate 16 g, Dietary fiber 2 g, Sugars 2 g, Protein 3 g, Vitamin A 2%, Vitamin C 1%, Calcium 10%, Iron 7%

Topping Nutrition Facts (1 serving = 1/6 recipe)

Calories 189, Fat 1 g, Saturated fat 0 g, Trans fat 0 g, Cholesterol 0 mg, Sodium 20 mg, Carbohydrate 47 g, Dietary fiber 2 g, Protein 2 g, Protein 2 g, Vitamin A 4%, Vitamin C 95%, Calcium 3%, Iron 6%

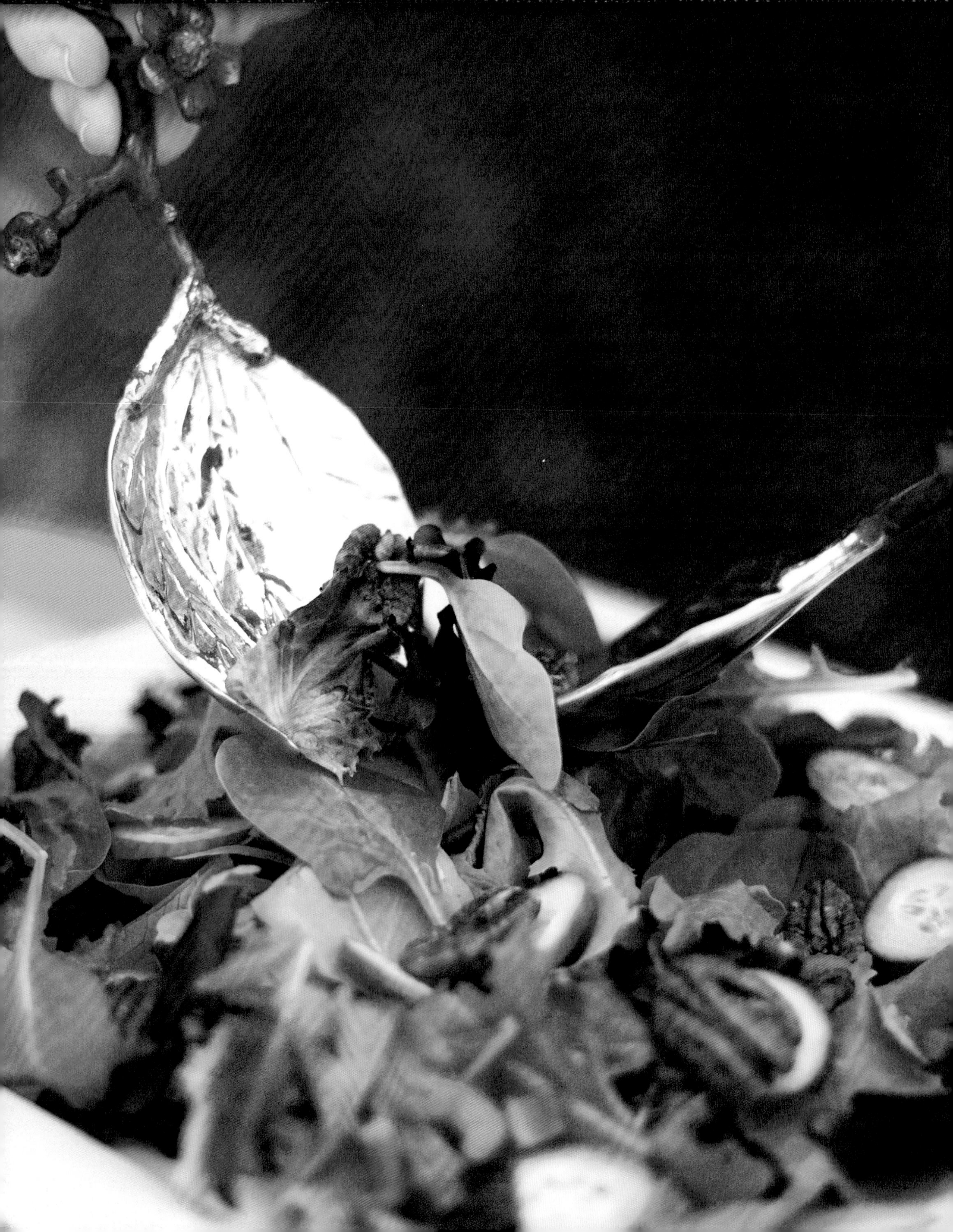

Mixed Greens Salad

Salad

1 bag mixed greens

2 Persian cucumbers, sliced

4 small yellow and/or orange bell peppers, sliced

¼ C dried black figs, diced

¼ C candied pecans

1 Bartlett pear, peeled and thinly sliced

Dressing

4 Tbs olive oil

2 ½ Tbs lemon juice, freshly squeezed

Salt to taste

In a salad platter combine greens, cucumbers, bell peppers, and figs. Just before serving, add lemon juice, olive oil, and salt to taste and toss. Sprinkle pecans on salad and place thin slices of pear on top. Enjoy! Serves 4-6.

Nutrition Facts (1 serving = 1/8 recipe)

Calories 206, Fat 15 g, Saturated 2 g, Polyunsaturated 3 g, Monounsaturated 9 g, Trans fat 0 g, Cholesterol 0 mg, Sodium 30 mg, Potassium 342 mg, Carbohydrate 20 g, Dietary fiber 4 g, Sugars 12 g, Protein 2 g, Vitamin A 74%, Vitamin C 137%, Calcium 4 %, Iron 7%

Black-Eyed Pea Salad

1-lb bag black-eyed peas

1 avocado, cubed

1 medium green pepper, chopped

½ C red onion, chopped

½ bunch cilantro without stems, chopped

Dressing

¼ C olive oil

¼ C fresh lemon or lime juice

1 clove fresh garlic

1 tsp salt

Soak black-eyed peas and cook until tender. Add remaining vegetables. Blend dressing ingredients in blender, then toss with the black-eyed pea salad. Serves 8. (I put the black-eyed peas in a crock-pot overnight on low)

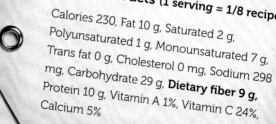

Nutrition Facts (1 serving = 1/8 recipe)

Calories 230, Fat 10 g, Saturated 2 g, Polyunsaturated 1 g, Monounsaturated 7 g, Trans fat 0 g, Cholesterol 0 mg, Sodium 298 mg, Carbohydrate 29 g, **Dietary fiber 9 g,** Protein 10 g, Vitamin A 1%, Vitamin C 24%, Calcium 5%

Bow Tie Pasta With Avocado

Salad

1 12 oz bow tie pasta

½ Tbs olive oil

2 avocados, diced

3 large Roma tomatoes, diced

2 green onions, chopped

4 - 5 Tbs fresh basil, chopped

Dressing

½ C olive oil

½ C fresh lemon juice

2 tsp salt

2 tsp oregano

2 tsp garlic powder

In a large pot bring salted water to a boil. Add the pasta and cook until done. Rinse pasta in cool water and drain. Add ½ Tbs olive oil and stir gently. Transfer to a serving platter.

Mix diced tomatoes, chopped green onions, diced avocados, and fresh basil, and pour some of the dressing over the vegetables. Pour avocado mixture over the pasta and toss gently. Add more dressing as desired. Delicious!

Salad yields 6 servings. Dressing yields 1 C or 8 servings (2 Tbs).

Using whole grain pasta will boost the fiber.

This recipe is adapted from the book
Depression, the Way Out, by Neil Nedley, MD.

Nutrition Facts (1 serving = 1/6 recipe)
Calories 327, Protein 8 g, Fat 12 g, Carbohydrate 46 g, Dietary fiber 5 g, Calcium 10 mg, Iron 7 mg, Sodium 9 mg

Dressing (1 serving = 2 Tbs) Calories 127, Fat 13.5 g, Carbohydrate 2 g, Calcium 8 mg, Sodium 582 mg

Brazilian Salad

3 - 4 cucumbers, peeled & chopped

3 - 4 tomatoes, chopped

½ bunch cilantro, chopped

1 bunch green onions, chopped

3 - 4 hearts of palm, chopped

Juice of 1 lime

1 - 2 Tbs extra virgin olive oil

3 - 4 cloves of fresh crushed garlic

½ tsp salt or to taste

Mix in a bowl and serve. Serves 8.

Hint: Hearts of palm come in a can and can be found in most grocery stores.

Nutrition Facts (1 serving = 1/8 recipe)

Calories 87, Fat 3 g, Saturated fat .5 g, Monounsaturated 2 g, Cholesterol 0 mg, Sodium 254 mg, Carbohydrate 13 g, Dietary fiber 3 g, Sugars 0 g, Protein 3 g, Vitamin A 14%, Vitamin C 34%, Calcium 7%, Iron 12%

Broccoli Salad

4 C broccoli heads, cut into small chunks

½ C chopped onions

1 C raisins

1 C lightly salted Spanish peanuts

Dressing

½ C organic sugar

1 C Vegenaise or mayo

2 Tbs lemon juice

If you make this salad ahead of time, don't add the dressing until ready to serve.

If serving the salad the same day, add the dressing 2 hours before, so the flavors can soak in. Just before serving, add the raisins and peanuts. Makes 4-6 servings.

Hint: I usually double this recipe, because it's so delicious it goes fast!

Nutrition Facts (1 serving = 1/5 recipe)

Calories 638, Fat 44 g, Saturated 4 g, Trans fat 0 g, Cholesterol 0 mg, Sodium 403 mg, Carbohydrate 56 g, Dietary fiber 4 g, Protein 11 g, Vitamin A 12%, Vitamin C 77%, Calcium 8%, Iron 10%

Cabbage Salad

1 head of cabbage, chopped

1 bunch of cilantro without stems, chopped

1 bunch chopped green onions

¾ C pine nuts

Juice of one lime

Salt to taste

Extra-light olive oil

Sauté pine nuts in extra-light olive oil until lightly browned. Sprinkle pine nuts with salt to taste. Combine all ingredients and drizzle with extra-light olive oil. Then squeeze the juice of a fresh lime over all.

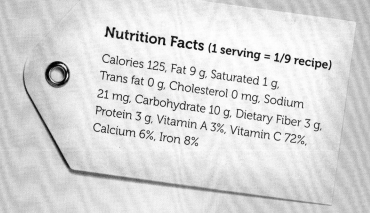

Nutrition Facts (1 serving = 1/9 recipe)
Calories 125, Fat 9 g, Saturated 1 g, Trans fat 0 g, Cholesterol 0 mg, Sodium 21 mg, Carbohydrate 10 g, Dietary Fiber 3 g, Protein 3 g, Vitamin A 3%, Vitamin C 72%, Calcium 6%, Iron 8%

Coleslaw

Slaw

1 medium sized cabbage, chopped

1 - 2 shredded carrots

½ chopped onion

Dressing

3 - 5 Tbs Vegenaise

½ tsp salt

¼ tsp garlic powder

¼ tsp onion powder or a little more

Drizzle of olive oil

1 tsp lemon juice (fresh is best)

Add 1 - 2 Tbs water to thin it down

Mix dressing and pour over coleslaw.
Mix thoroughly. Garnish with extra carrot shreds.
Serves 6.

Nutrition Facts (1 serving = 1/6 recipe)

Calories 114, Fat 7 g, Saturated 1 g,
Trans fat 0 g, Cholesterol 0 mg, Sodium
287 mg, Carbohydrate 12 g, Dietary fiber 4 g,
Protein 2 g, Vitamin A 23%, Vitamin C 106%,
Calcium 8%, Iron 6%

Creamed Cucumbers

7 pickling cucumbers

½ tub Follow Your Heart sour cream

½ to 1 Tbs fresh dill weed, finely chopped

½ tsp salt or to taste

Slice cucumbers into thin slices. Mix in the Follow Your Heart sour cream and dill weed. Add salt to taste. Serves 4-6. My Mom made this recipe when I was growing up. A Polish favorite of ours!

Nutrition Facts (1 serving = 1/5 recipe)

Calories 120, Fat 6 g, Saturated 2 g, Trans fat 0 g, Cholesterol 0 mg, Sodium 427 mg, Carbohydrate 15 g, Dietary fiber 1 g, Protein 2 g, Vitamin A 1%, Vitamin C 5%, Calcium 2%, Iron 2%

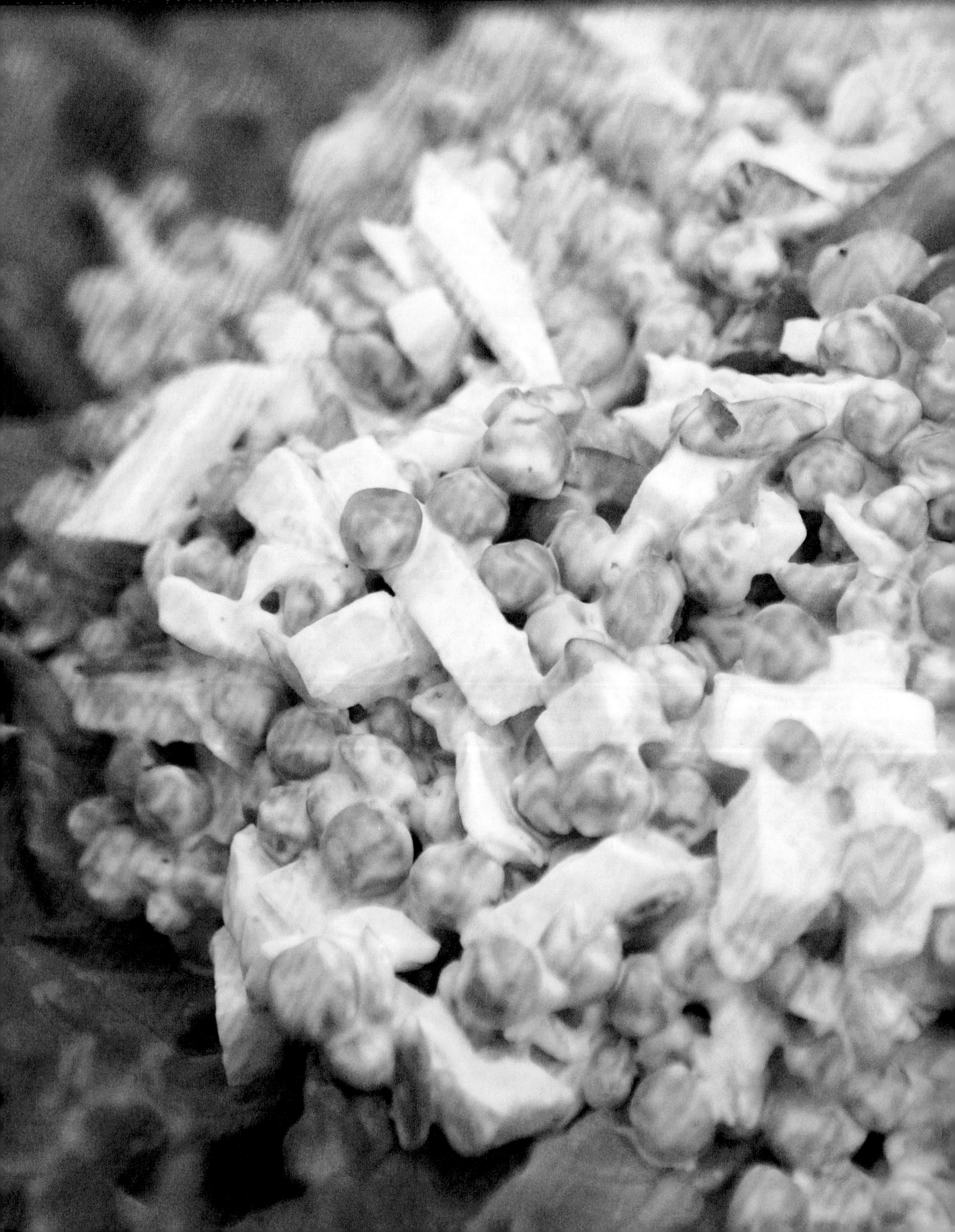

Peas & Peanuts Salad

3 C peas, frozen

½ C onion, chopped

1 C jicama, sliced julienne style

½ C peanuts, dry-roasted, unsalted

¼ C sunflower seeds, dry-roasted, unsalted

¼ C pumpkin seeds

4 leaves romaine lettuce

1 Tbs green onion, chopped

1 cup Vegenaise or mayo

¼ tsp garlic salt

½ tsp onion salt

½ tsp Mrs. Dash Salt-Free Garlic and Herb Seasoning

Defrost one bag of frozen peas. Mix the peas, onions, and jicama together. Mix the peanuts, sunflower seeds, and pumpkin seeds together. Mix the Vegenaise, garlic salt, onion salt and Mrs. Dash Garlic and Herb Seasoning. Put the Romaine lettuce leaves or leaf lettuce on a plate.
When ready to serve, mix all the ingredients together and put in a mound on the lettuce.

Hint: If you want to make this ahead, don't add the seeds until ready to serve, or they won't be crisp.

Nutrition Facts (1 serving = 1/8 recipe)

Calories 341, Fat 27 g, Saturated 2 g, Trans fat 0 g, Cholesterol 0 mg, Sodium 389 mg, Carbohydrate 17 g, **Dietary fiber 6 g,** Protein 8 g, Vitamin A 9%, Vitamin C 16%, Calcium 4%, Iron 135

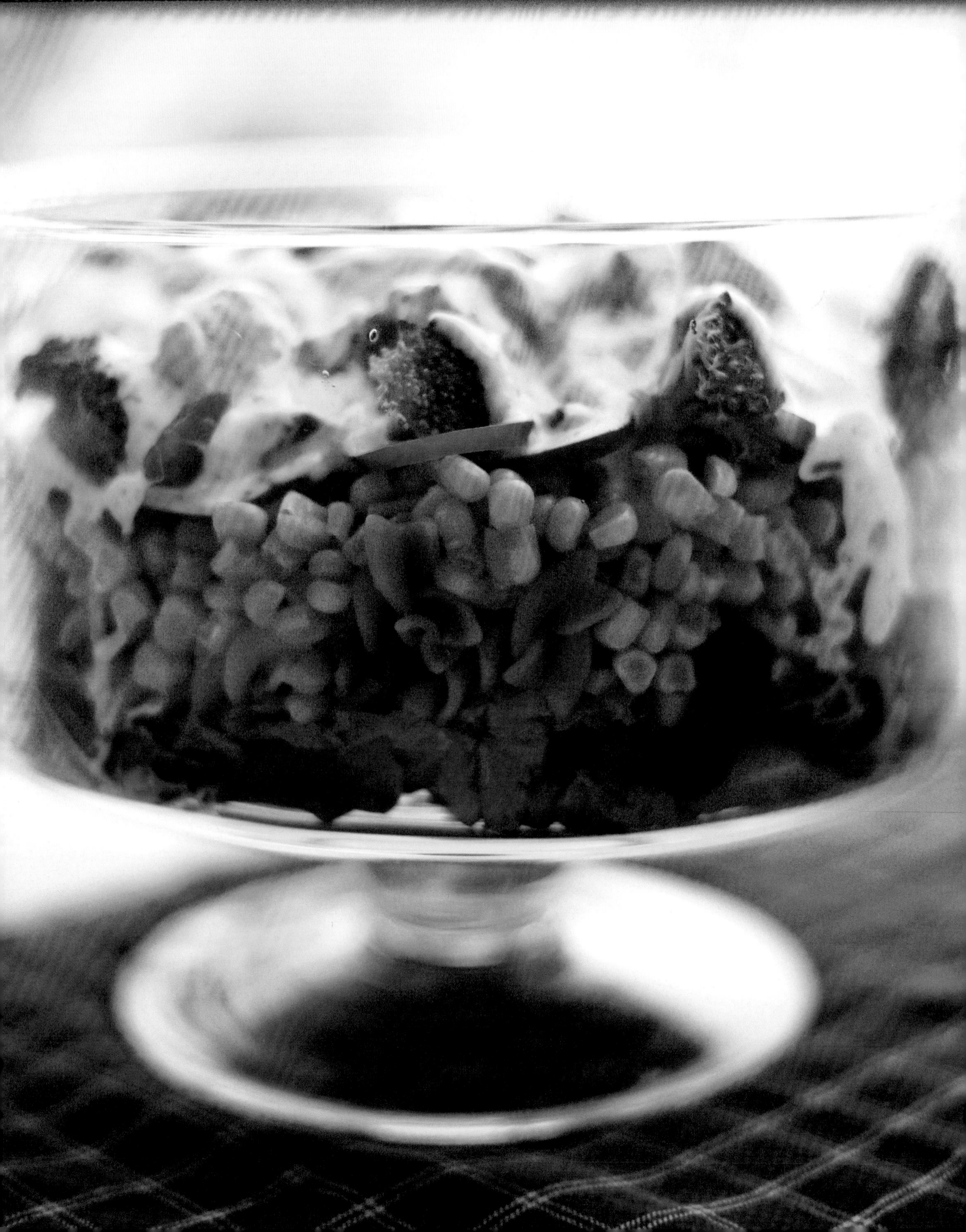

Seven-Layer Salad

Layer the following in a large glass bowl:

4 C assorted salad greens or leaf lettuce

1 C shredded carrots

2 C cooked tri-color pasta (or elbow pasta)

2 C frozen organic corn, defrosted, rinsed in colander

1 C sliced red bell pepper

2 C chopped tomatoes

1 C broccoli florets

½ - 1 C jicama, sliced julienne style

Nutrition Facts (1 serving = 1/6 recipe)
Calories 376, Fat 25 g, Saturated 2 g,
Trans fat 0 g, Cholesterol 0 mg,
Sodium 433 mg, Carbohydrate 32 g,
Dietary fiber 5 g, Protein 5 g,
Vitamin A 66%, Vitamin C 75%,
Calcium 4%, Iron 9%

Dressing

1 to 1 ½ C Vegenaise or mayo

½ tsp salt

1 ½ tsp basil

2 - 3 Tbs water, or more if needed

Mix the dressing and spoon on top of salad. If using a large bowl, you will need the 1 ½ C of Vegenaise.

This is a delicious salad, colorful and full of nutritious vegetables. You can use other vegetables for variety. Serves 6.

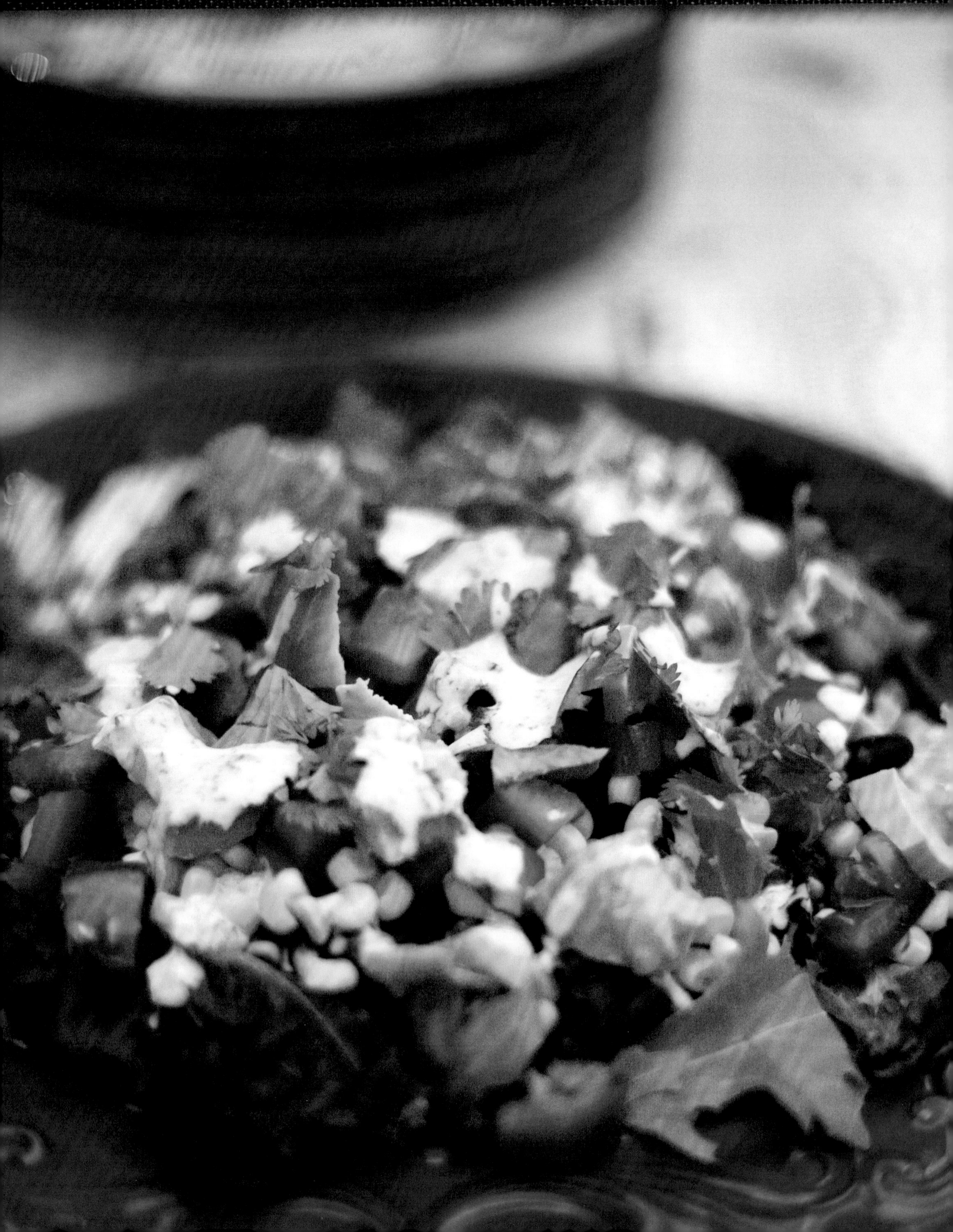

Southwest Salad

1 bag mixed salad greens (or 3 - 4 C)

1 can black beans, drained and rinsed

2 tomatoes, chopped

1 red bell pepper, chopped

2 C frozen organic corn, thawed or fresh kernels

1 avocado, chopped

¼ C cilantro, chopped

Layer ingredients in order listed. Top with salsa or drizzle ranch dressing on top. Serves 4.

Hint: You can also add sliced olives to this.

Nutrition Facts (1 serving = ¼ recipe)

Calories 253, Fat 9 g, Saturated 1 g, Trans fat 0 g, Cholesterol 0 mg, Sodium 470 mg, Carbohydrate 43 g, Protein 12 g, **Dietary Fiber 11 g,** Vitamin A 58%, Vitamin C 77%, Calcium 9%, Iron 20%

Spinach Salad

Salad

Wash two bags of baby spinach leaves

1 can mandarin oranges or fresh oranges

1 bunch of green onions, chopped

Caramelized Almonds

¼ C slivered almonds

3 Tbs organic sugar

Combine almonds and sugar in dry skillet, cook slowly and keep stirring until brown and caramelized. Stir as it cools to separate.

Hint: You can use plain slivered almonds if you wish; caramelizing them makes it more crunchy and sweet.

Dressing

1/3 C lemon juice

½ C olive oil

1 Tbs organic sugar

1 tsp parsley flakes

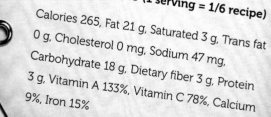

Nutrition Facts (1 serving = 1/6 recipe)

Calories 265, Fat 21 g, Saturated 3 g, Trans fat 0 g, Cholesterol 0 mg, Sodium 47 mg, Carbohydrate 18 g, Dietary fiber 3 g, Protein 3 g, Vitamin A 133%, Vitamin C 78%, Calcium 9%, Iron 15%

Combine all just before serving.

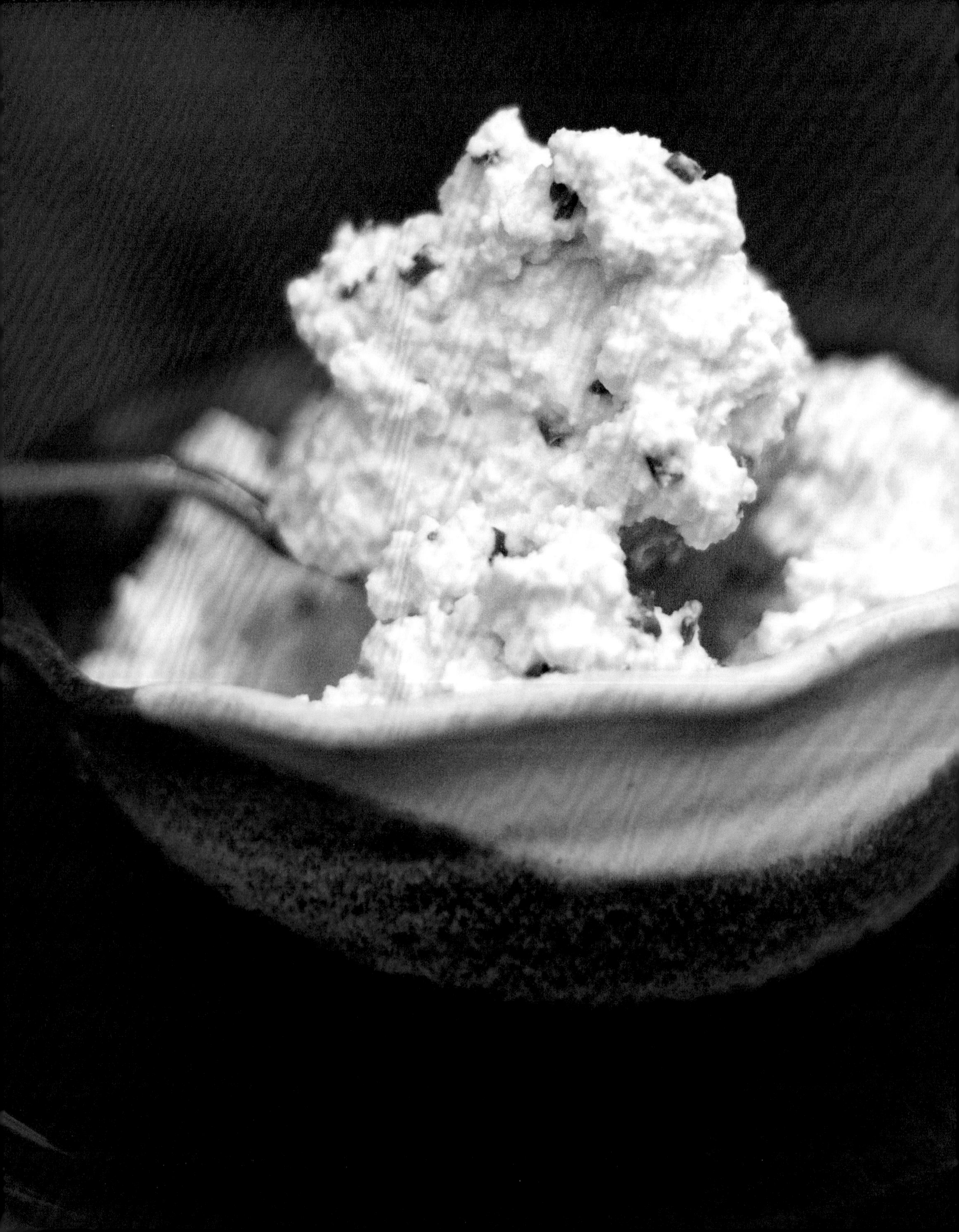

Tofu Cottage Cheese

4 C organic tofu, extra firm, water packed

2 ¼ tsp onion powder

¾ C Follow Your Heart sour cream

¼ tsp citric acid or 1 - 2 Tbs lemon juice

1 ½ tsp salt

½ tsp garlic salt

2 Tbs chives

Squeeze excess water out of the tofu by pressing tofu block between your hands. Crumble tofu in a bowl and add seasonings. Add citric acid to Follow Your Heart sour cream. Stir into tofu mixture. Mix in the chives. Makes 4 C. This recipe is from the Lifestyle Center of America.

Nutrition Facts (1 serving = 1/15 recipe)

Calories 91, Fat 6 g, Saturated 1 g, Trans fat 0 g, Cholesterol 0 mg, Sodium 367 mg, Carbohydrate 5 g, Dietary fiber 0 g, Protein 6 g, Vitamin A 0%, Vitamin C 2%, Calcium 11% , Iron 6%

Tofu Lettuce Wraps

Lettuce Wraps

2 ½ C organic tofu, extra firm, water-packed, cut into ¼ inch cubes

½ C meatless burger crumbles (Morningstar Farms, freezer section)

1 Tbs vegetarian chicken style seasoning

1 - 2 tsp extra virgin olive oil	½ C onion, chopped
4 green onions, minced	2 garlic cloves, minced
2 Tbs toasted sesame oil	2 Tbs light organic soy sauce
2 Tbs honey	Dash of cayenne pepper (optional)

Sauté onion, green onions, garlic, tofu cubes, and burger crumbles in olive oil until the tofu is browned. Add remaining ingredients and cook for 4 - 5 minutes longer. Remove from the heat and allow to cool before filling the lettuce leaves. For these wraps, iceburg lettuce leaves work best. Use about ¼ C of the tofu mixture and put in the lettuce leaf and top with 1 - 2 Tbs peanut sauce. You can hold the wrap together with a toothpick. Makes 4 C (16 – ¼ C servings)

Nutrition Facts (1 serving = ¼ C)

Calories 113, Fat 8.2 g, Carbohydrate 4.8 g, Protein 7 g, Dietary fiber 1.1 g, Sodium 206 mg

Peanut Sauce

1 can light coconut milk	½ tsp salt
¾ C creamy peanut butter	1/3 C organic sugar or more to taste
1 - 2 Tbs fresh lemon juice	1/8 tsp red curry paste (optional)
¼ C water	

Nutrition Facts: (1 serving = 1/32 recipe)

Calories 53, Fat 4 g, Saturated 1 g, Trans fat 0 g, Cholesterol 0 mg, Sodium 66 mg, Carbohydrate 3 g, Dietary fiber 0 g, Protein 2 g, Vitamin A 1%, Vitamin C 1%, Calcium 1%, Iron 2%.

Heat coconut milk in a kettle on low until it simmers. Then add peanut butter, sucanat, salt, and red curry paste. Simmer on low heat until sauce is well blended and begins to thicken.

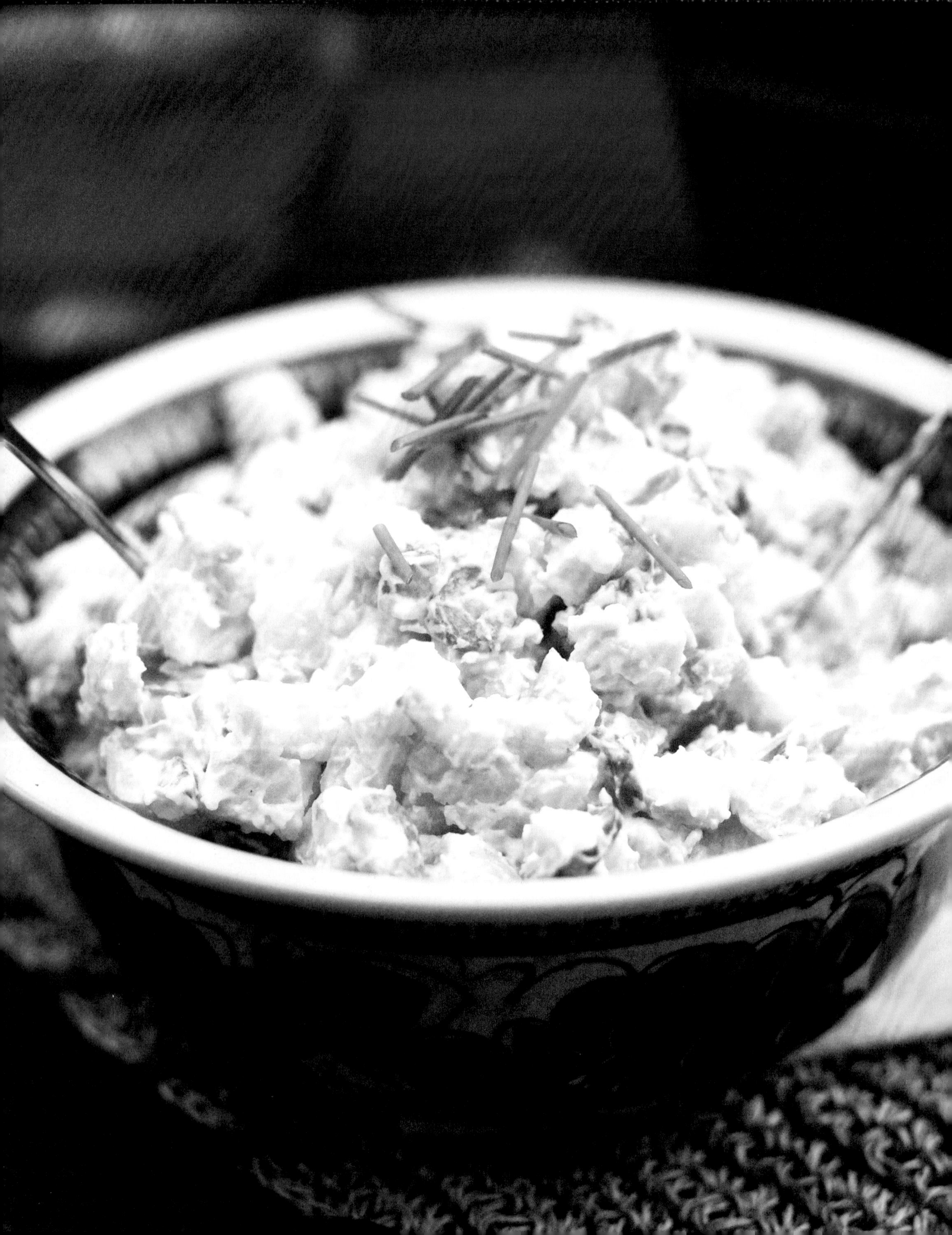

Potato Salad

4 - 5 potatoes, peeled, cooked, and cubed

¾ C sliced green olives

4 green onions, chopped

2 pickles, diced (I prefer Bubbies brand)

1 carrot, shredded

4 - 5 heaping Tbs Vegenaise or mayo

Salt to taste

Cube cooked potatoes. Add olives, green onions, carrot, and pickles. Stir in Vegenaise to moisten. Makes 6 servings.

Bubbie's pickles are found in the refrigerator section of a health food store. They are made with salt, garlic, dill, and spices. Very tasty.

Nutrition Facts (1 serving = 1/6 recipe)

Calories 197, Fat 9 g, Saturated Fat 0 g,
Trans fat 0 g, Cholesterol 0 mg,
Sodium 284 mg, Carbohydrate 28 g,
Dietary fiber 3 g, Protein 3 g, Vitamin A 41%,
Vitamin C 23%, Calcium 2%, Iron 4%

Veggie Lettuce Wraps

Romaine lettuce leaves

2 - 3 thinly sliced radishes

2 thinly sliced summer squash

1 red bell pepper, sliced in thin strips

1 avocado, diced

1 carrot, shredded

½ bunch cilantro, chopped

1 cucumber, chopped

Nutrition Facts (1 serving = 1/3 recipe)

Calories 262, Fat 19 g, Saturated 2 g,
Trans fat 0 g, Cholesterol 0 mg,
Sodium 213 mg, Carbohydrate 20 g,
Dietary Fiber 9 g, Protein 5 g, Vitamin A 155%,
Vitamin C 153%, Calcium 7%, Iron 10%

Put chopped veggies in a romaine lettuce leaf and top with ranch dressing.
Makes 2 - 4 lettuce wraps.

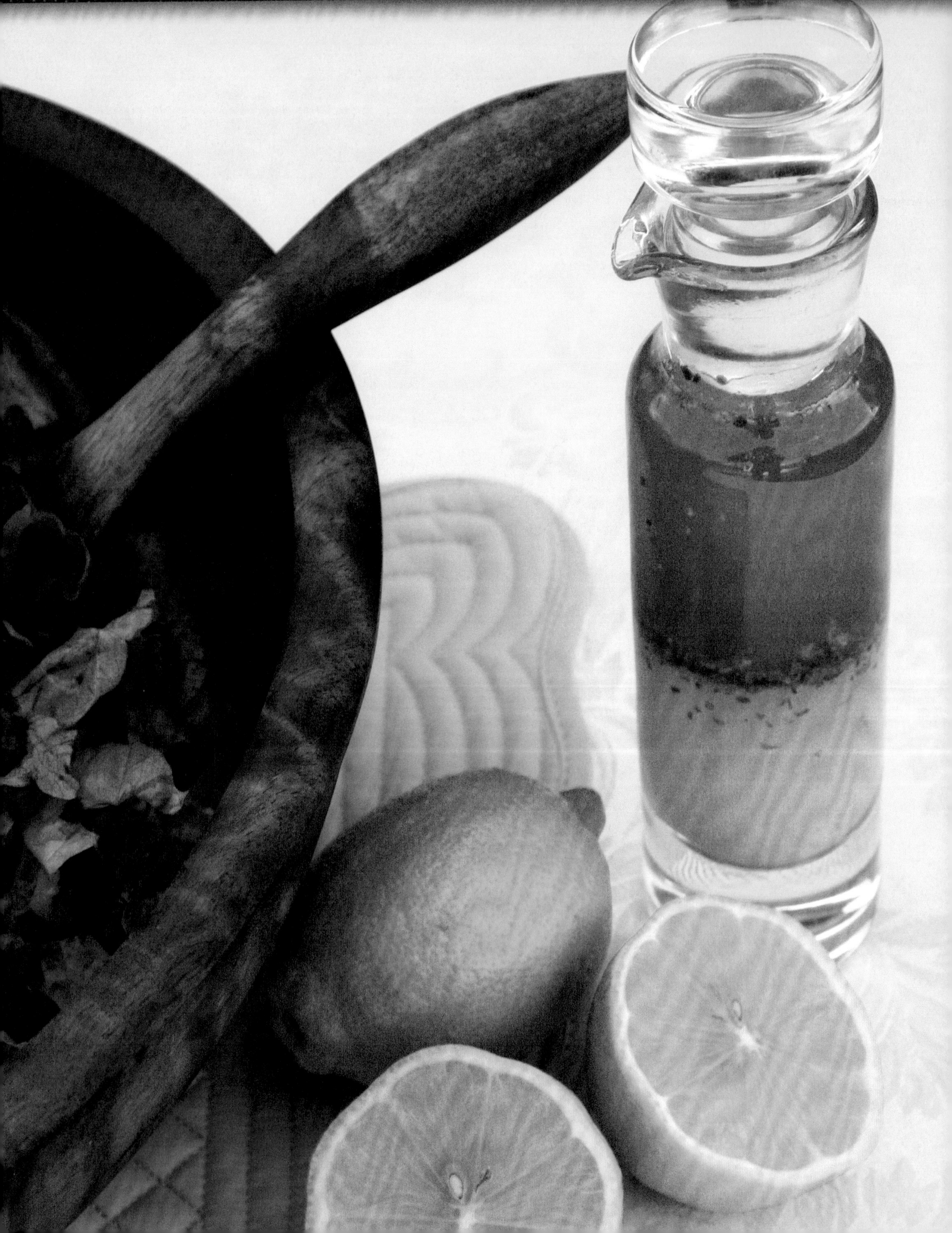

Salad Dressing

¼ C olive oil

¼ C fresh lemon juice

1 tsp salt

1 tsp garlic powder

1 tsp oregano

Mix all ingredients. If making ahead of time, you refrigerate it and then take it out soon enough so it will thin back down. The olive oil thickens when refrigerated.

Nutrition Facts (1 serving = 2 Tbs = ¼ recipe)

Calories 125, Fat 14 g, Saturated 2 g,
Polyunsaturated 2 g, Monounsaturated 10 g,
Trans fat 0 g, Cholesterol 0 mg,
Sodium 582 mg, Carbohydrate 2 g,
Dietary fiber 0 g, Protein 0 g, Vitamin A 1%,
Vitamin C 10%, Calcium 1%, Iron 2%

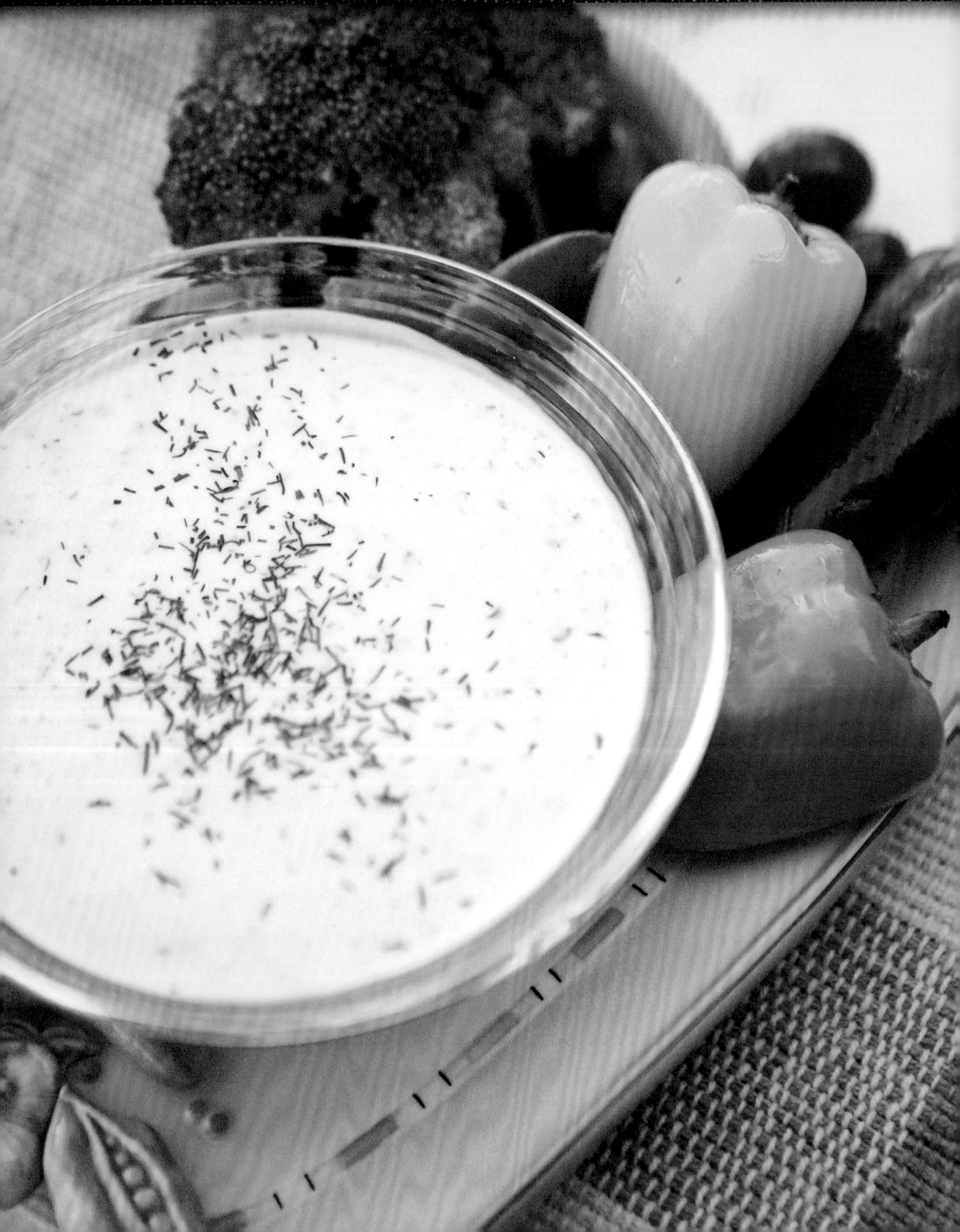

Ranch Dressing

1 C Vegenaise or mayo

1 tsp dill weed

1 tsp garlic powder

1 tsp onion powder

1 Tbs parsley

½ tsp salt

1/8 tsp paprika (optional)

1 tsp lemon juice

¼ C water or organic unsweetened soymilk

Mix thoroughly, and if it's too thick, add a little more water or soymilk.

Note: Nutrition Facts are for dressing made with water.

Nutrition Facts (1 serving = 1/15 recipe)

Calories 97, Fat 10 g, Saturated 1 g, Trans fat 0 g, Cholesterol 0 mg, Sodium 165 mg, Carbohydrate 1 g, Dietary fiber 0 g, Protein 1 g, Vitamin A 1%, Vitamin C 1%, Calcium 1%, Iron 2%

Tomato Florentine Soup

1 medium onion chopped

2 cloves garlic, minced

1 Tbs olive oil

2 1-lb cans tomato sauce, low sodium

1 16 oz can diced tomatoes

1 bay leaf

2/3 – 1 C organic soy creamer or ½ C raw cashews,
   blended in 1 C water

1 Tbs organic sugar

1 tsp oregano

1 tsp basil

1 tsp garlic powder

1 tsp onion powder

2 C washed and chopped spinach

Sauté onion and garlic in olive oil in a kettle. Add tomatoes, tomato sauce, and seasonings. Simmer for ½ hour. Remove bay leaf and add spinach. Cook another 5 minutes. Serves 6.

Nutrition Facts (1 serving = 1/6 recipe)

Calories 150, Fat 7 g, Saturated 1 g,
Trans fat 0 g, Cholesterol 0 mg,
Sodium 343 mg, Carbohydrate 21 g,
Dietary Fiber 4 g, Protein 4 g, Vitamin A 57%,
Vitamin C 42%, Calcium 7%, Iron 12%

Easy Chili

4 15-oz cans of chili beans (or you can use 2 cans chili beans / 2 cans small red beans)

¼ tsp onion powder

½ tsp fresh garlic minced

¼ tsp salt-free Frontier-brand Mexican seasoning

Optional Additions:

¼ tsp Tony's seasoning

¼ tsp hickory liquid smoke

1/8 tsp crushed, dried, red chili peppers

Combine all ingredients and cook on the stove, or put in the crock-pot overnight.

Also, you can sauté Morningstar Farms frozen burger crumbles in a little olive oil with chopped onions and add this to your chili. Another option is to add a can of petite diced tomatoes.

Hint: The USDA ranks the small red bean to have the highest antioxidant capacity.

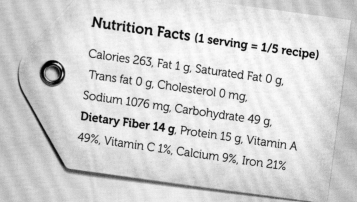

Nutrition Facts (1 serving = 1/5 recipe)

Calories 263, Fat 1 g, Saturated Fat 0 g, Trans fat 0 g, Cholesterol 0 mg, Sodium 1076 mg, Carbohydrate 49 g, **Dietary Fiber 14 g**, Protein 15 g, Vitamin A 49%, Vitamin C 1%, Calcium 9%, Iron 21%

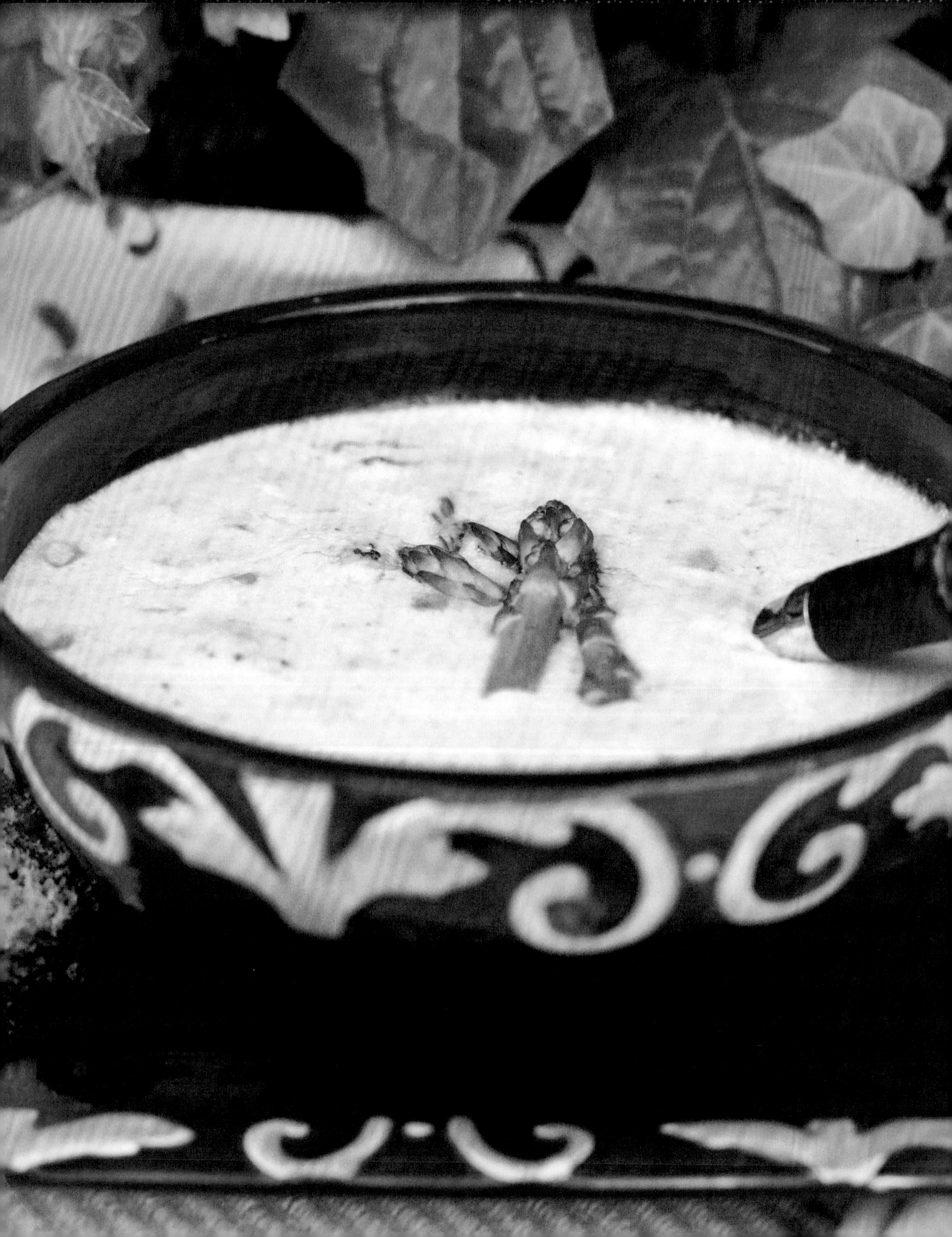

Cream of Fresh Vegetable Soup

1 ½ C chopped fresh vegetables (i.e.: peas, broccoli, asparagus)

1 Tbs olive oil

½ C onion, chopped

¼ C celery, diced

¼ C carrot, shredded

1 C fresh vegetables, diced

> (I use about ¾ C asparagus and make the other ¼ C
> with the other vegetables—love asparagus)

4 C water

2/3 C raw cashews

2 Tbs chicken style seasoning

1 tsp salt

½ tsp onion powder

¼ tsp celery salt

Steam 1 ½ C vegetables in a small amount of water until cooked. Place steamed vegetables in the blender and blend until smooth. Put blended vegetables in a bowl. Pour olive oil in a kettle and sauté onion, celery, and carrot. Then add 3 C of water and bring to a slow boil. Add blended vegetables and 1 C of diced fresh vegetables. Simmer for 5 minutes. Put cashews and 1 C of water and seasonings in the blender and blend until smooth. Slowly add to the soup and bring to a boil. This is a very tasty soup. Serves 4.

This recipe adapted from
The Best of Silver Hills Cookbook.

Nutrition Facts (1 serving = 1/4 recipe)

Calories 225, Fat 14 g, Saturated 3 g,
Polyunsaturated 2 g, Monounsaturated 9 g,
Trans fat 0 g, Cholesterol 0 mg,
Sodium 1300 mg, Carbohydrate 20 g,
Dietary fiber 4 g, Protein 7 g, Vitamin A 41%,
Vitamin C 35%, Calcium 5%, Iron 13%

Lentil Soup

1 C lentils

7 C water

½ C onion, chopped

2 stalks celery, chopped

2 bay leaves

½ tsp oregano

1 carrot, chopped

1 clove minced garlic

1 Tbs olive oil

1 can non-dairy tomato soup or tomato sauce

1 tsp salt

2 Tbs vegetarian chicken seasoning

Sauté vegetables in olive oil or a small amount of water. Rinse lentils. Combine all. Bring to a boil and simmer 30 - 45 minutes until done. You can add ½ C cooked brown rice to this to boost the fiber. You can also substitute tomato sauce if you don't have the tomato soup.
Makes 6 servings.

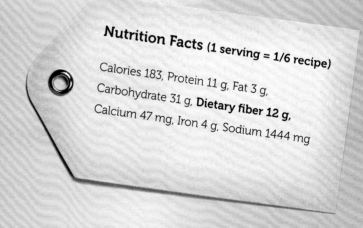

Nutrition Facts (1 serving = 1/6 recipe)

Calories 183, Protein 11 g, Fat 3 g,
Carbohydrate 31 g, **Dietary fiber 12 g,**
Calcium 47 mg, Iron 4 g, Sodium 1444 mg

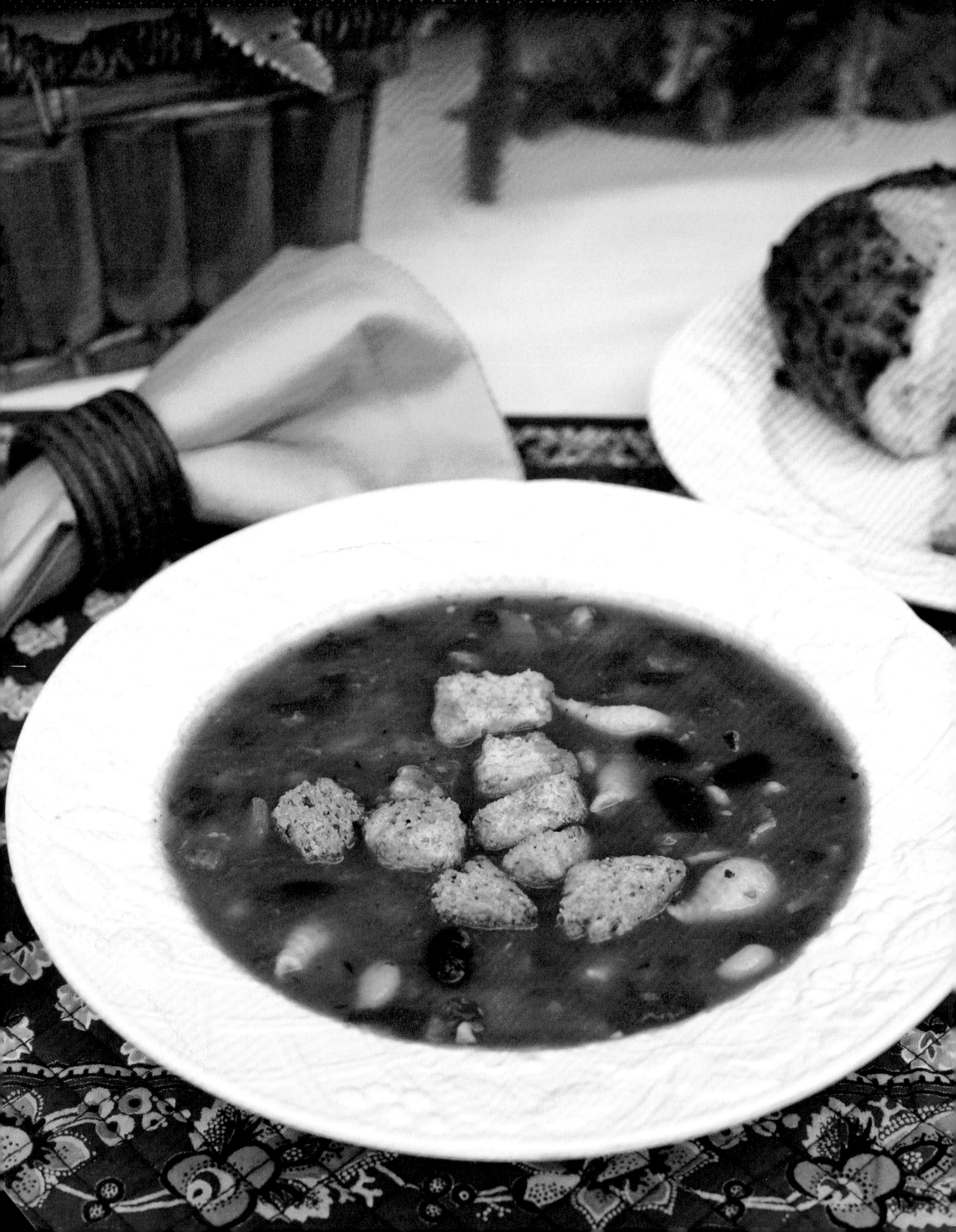

Minestrone Soup

2 Tbs olive oil

½ C celery, chopped

½ C zucchini, sliced

½ C onion, chopped

½ C frozen cut Italian green beans

4 cloves of minced garlic

1 ½ cubes Organic Gourmet vegetable bouillon

4 C hot water

2 cans kidney beans

1 can small white beans

1 can garbonzo beans

1 14-oz can diced tomatoes

½ C carrots, sliced

½ C favorite marinara sauce

2 C baby spinach, chopped

½ C small shell pasta

1 Tbs fresh parsley, chopped

1 tsp dried oregano

1 tsp salt

½ tsp dried sweet basil

¼ tsp thyme

Heat the olive oil in a large kettle. Sauté the garlic, onion, celery, green beans, and zucchini until tender. Next, add the bouillon cubes, hot water, tomatoes, beans, carrots, and spices. Bring the soup to a boil and then simmer for 20 minutes. Next add the pasta and spinach and cook for another 20 minutes. Serves 8.

Hint: You can use whole grain pasta and boost the fiber content.

Nutrition Facts (1 serving = 1/8 recipe)
Calories 260, Fat 5g, Saturated 1 g,
Polyunsaturated 1 g, Monounsaturated 3 g,
Trans fat 0 g, Cholesterol 0 mg,
Sodium 842 mg, Carbohydrate 43 g,
Dietary fiber 7 g, Protein 12 g, Vitamin A 46%,
Vitamin 18%, Calcium 12%, Iron 22%

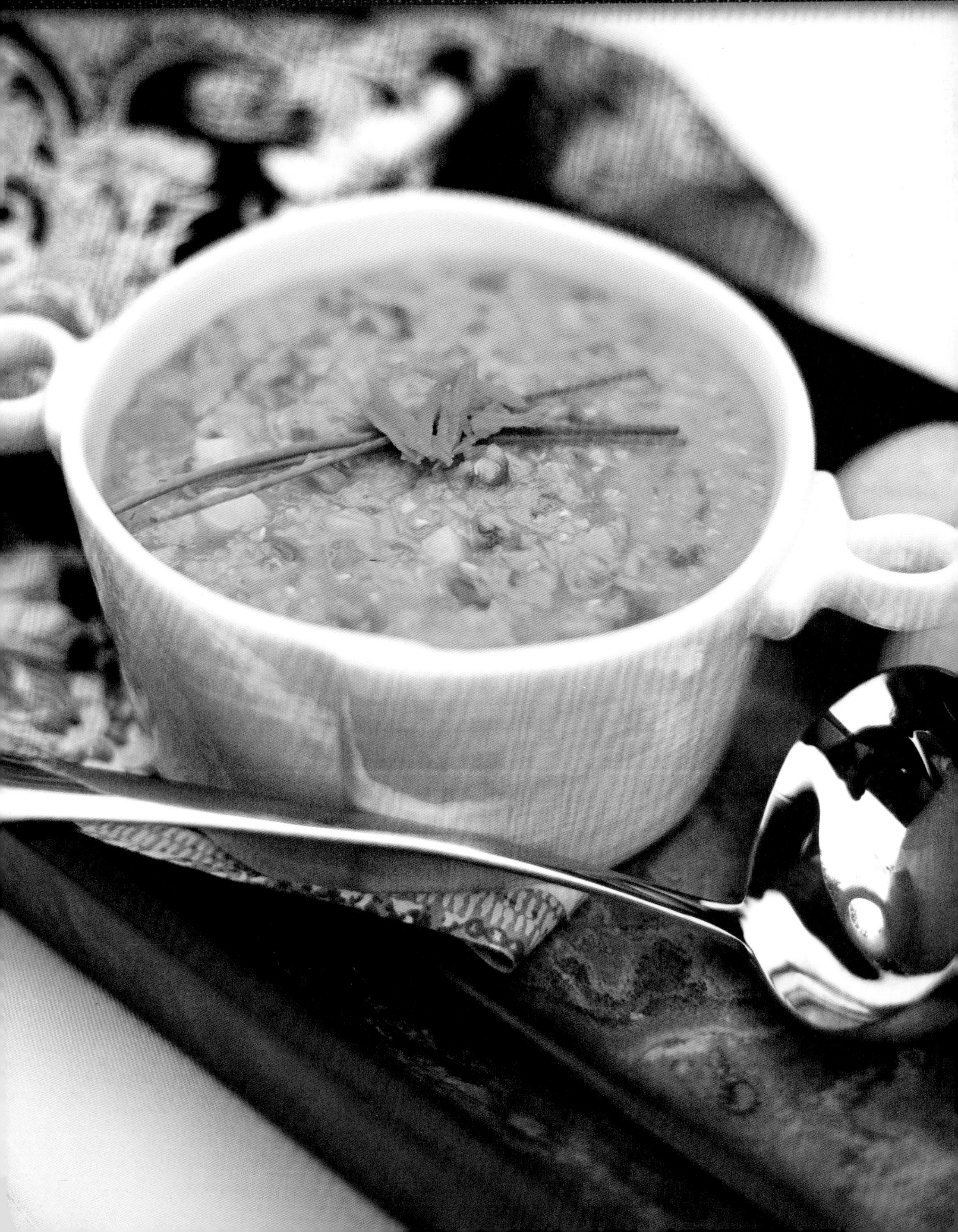

Red Lentil Soup

1 C red lentils

4 C water

½ - 1 tsp salt

1 parsnip, diced

14-oz can petite diced tomatoes

¼ C fresh cilantro, chopped

½ - 1 tsp Mrs. Dash Southwest Chipotle seasoning blend

1 - 2 Tbs olive oil

1 carrot, diced

½ C onion, chopped

2 - 3 cloves garlic, minced

1 Tbs lemon juice

1 vegetable bouillon cube

Rinse the lentils in cold water. Drain and place in a kettle with 4 C water and the bouillon cube. Bring to a boil and cook for about ½ hour or until tender.

Sauté the carrot, parsnip, garlic, and onion until tender. Add the diced tomatoes and Mrs. Dash seasoning. Add the vegetables and seasonings to the soup and cook a little longer. Remove kettle from the stove and add the lemon juice and chopped cilantro. Serves 3 - 4.

This soup is a family favorite!

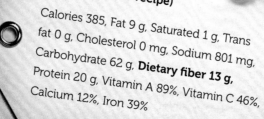

Nutrition Facts
(1 serving = 1/3 recipe)

Calories 385, Fat 9 g, Saturated 1 g, Trans fat 0 g, Cholesterol 0 mg, Sodium 801 mg, Carbohydrate 62 g, **Dietary fiber 13 g,** Protein 20 g, Vitamin A 89%, Vitamin C 46%, Calcium 12%, Iron 39%

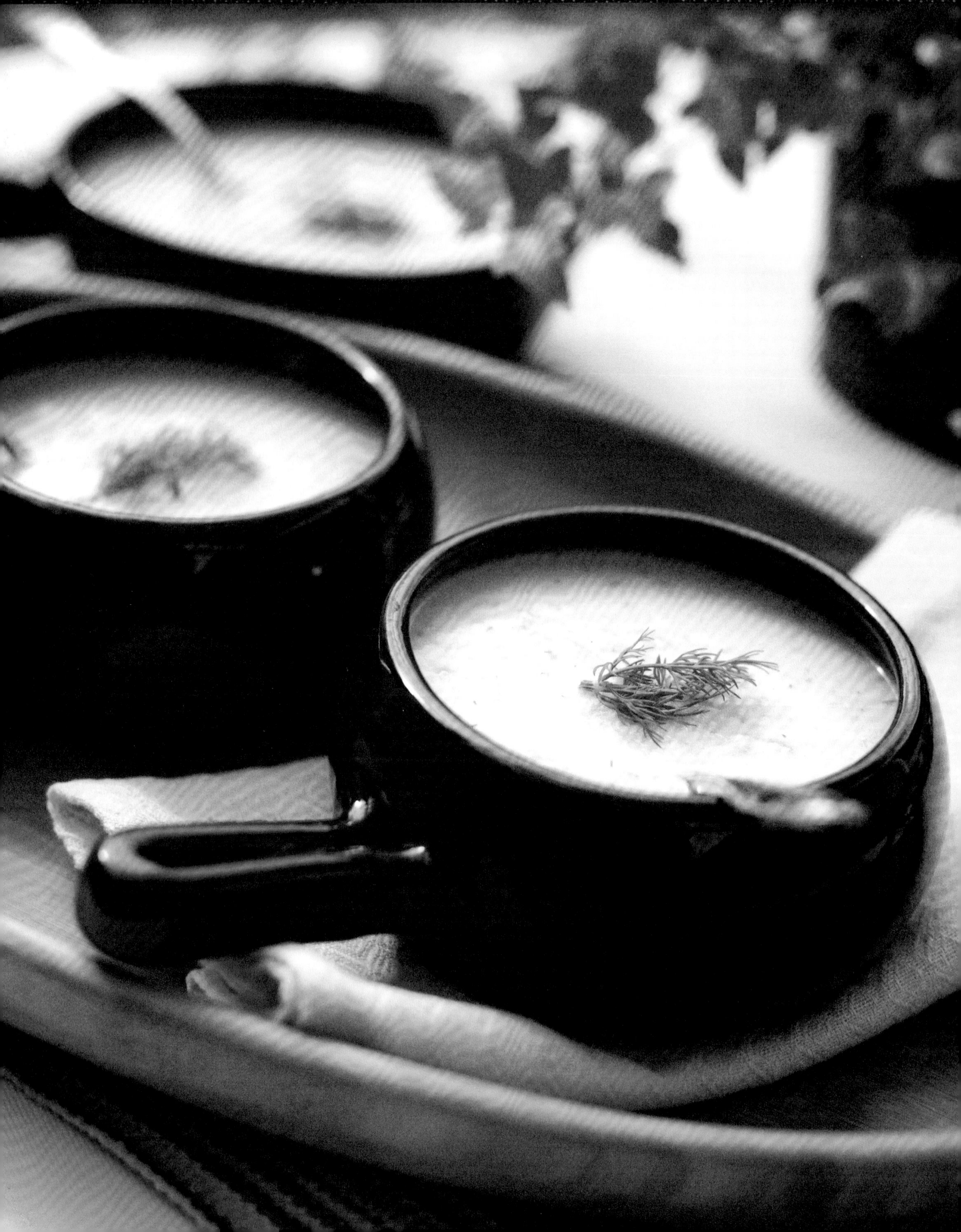

Potato Soup

½ C onion, chopped

1 C celery, chopped

½ tsp garlic powder

1 ½ tsp salt

4 - 6 peeled potatoes

4 C unsweetened organic soymilk

½ C Follow Your Heart sour cream

1 tsp dill weed

Combine the first 5 ingredients and cover with just enough water to cook. Before potatoes are completely done, mash them. Add the milk and cook a little more. Add the Follow Your Heart sour cream and dill weed. Serves 4 - 6.

Nutrition Facts (1 serving = 1/5 recipe)

Calories 231, Fat 8 g, Saturated 2 g,
Trans fat 0 g, Cholesterol 0 mg,
Sodium 838 mg, Carbohydrate 34 g,
Dietary fiber 5 g, Protein 9 g, Vitamin A 2%,
Vitamin C 34%, Calcium 4%, Iron 12%

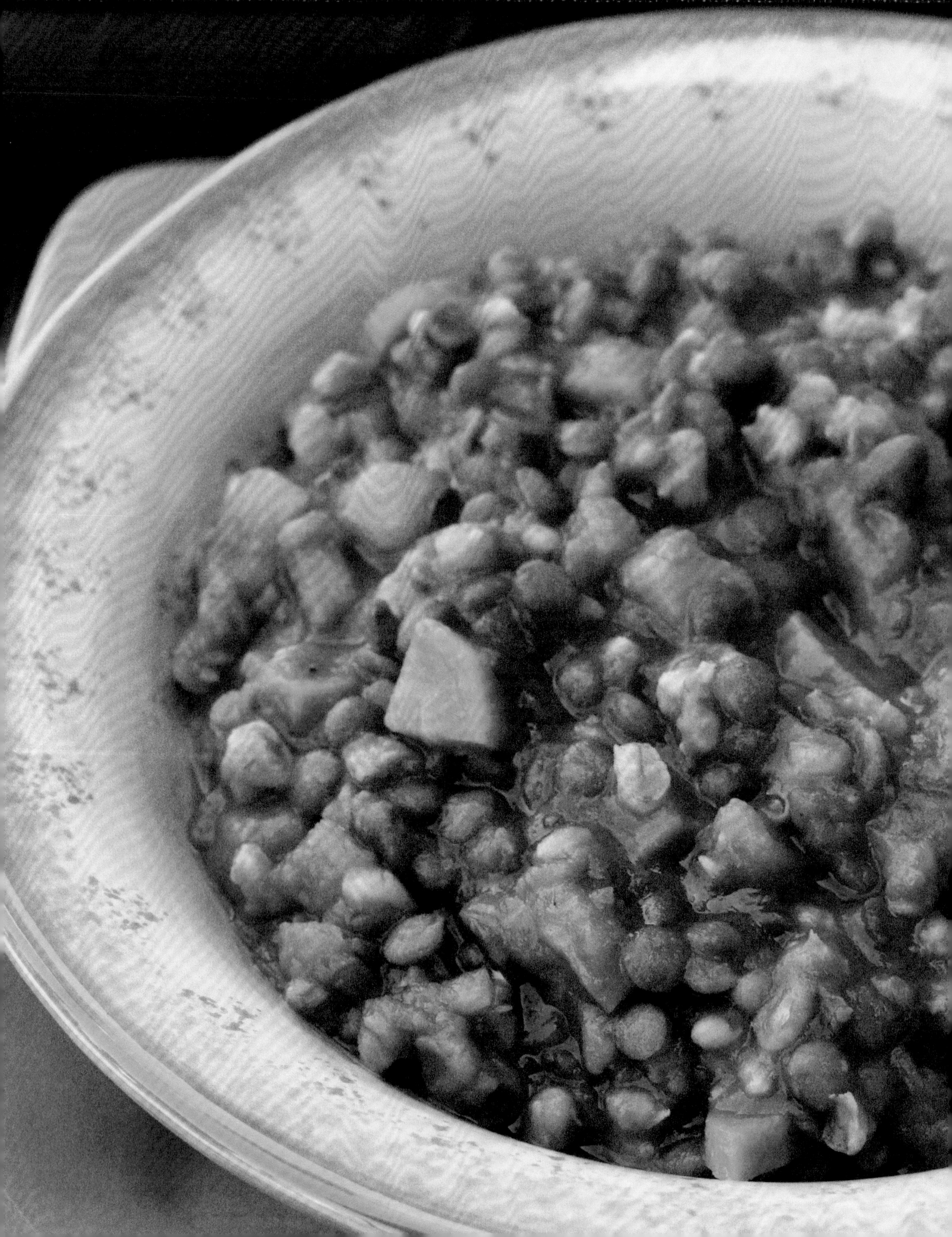

Lentil Stew

2 ½ quarts water

2 C lentils

1 C pearled barley

2 carrots, chopped

2 stalks celery, chopped

¼ C olive oil

½ C onion, chopped

1 can diced tomatoes

1 tsp salt

1 potato, cubed

½ - 1 C your favorite marinara sauce (optional)

Combine all ingredients in a large kettle and cook for 1 hour.

This soup is packed with fiber and nutrition!

Nutrition Facts (1 serving = 1/6 recipe)
Calories 421, Fat 4 g, Saturated 1 g,
Polyunsaturated 1 g, Monounsaturated 2 g,
Trans fat 0 g, Cholesterol 0 mg, Sodium 582 mg,
Potassium 989 mg, Carbohydrate 78 g,
Dietary Fiber 28 g (111%), Protein 22 g,
Vitamin A 38%, Vitamin C 24%, Calcium 9%,
Iron 35%

Split Pea Soup

1 C split peas

4 C water

1 tsp salt

1 onion, chopped

1 - 2 carrots, grated

2 bay leaves

1 - 2 tsp minced garlic

1 Tbs olive oil (optional)

Cook split peas in salted water until soft—about ½ hour. Add onion, carrots, etc. and continue cooking until they are tender. Thin with water if the soup gets too thick.
Remove bay leaves before serving.
Serves 4.

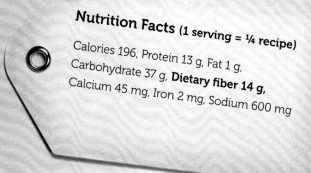

Nutrition Facts (1 serving = ¼ recipe)

Calories 196, Protein 13 g, Fat 1 g,
Carbohydrate 37 g, **Dietary fiber 14 g,**
Calcium 45 mg, Iron 2 mg, Sodium 600 mg

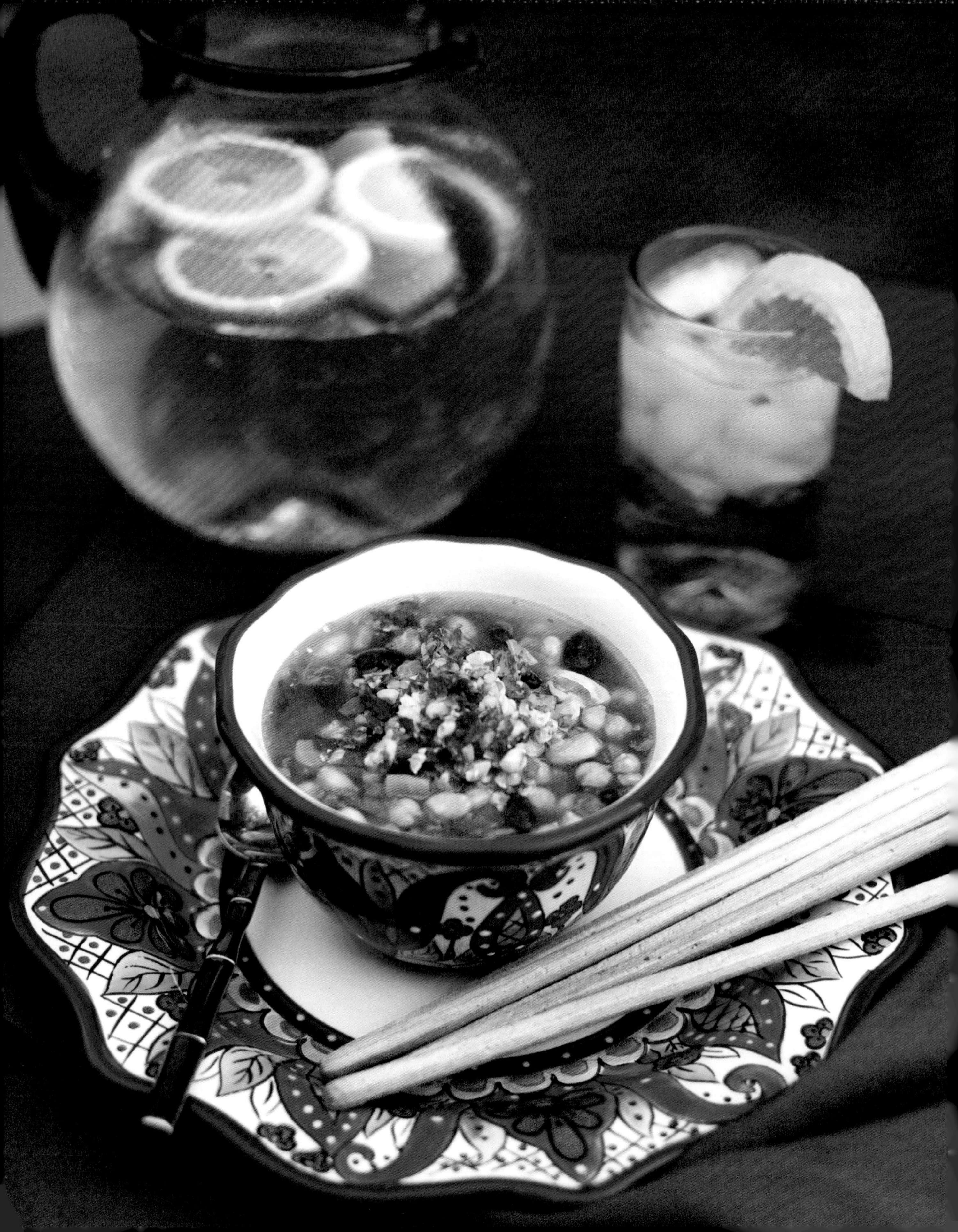

Chili With Pesto

3-Bean Chili

½ C onion, chopped

1 carrot, chopped

1 can diced tomatoes

1 can garbanzos

1 can cannellini beans

1 can kidney beans

1 tsp salt

2 C water

Pesto Sauce

3 cloves minced garlic

3 Tbs pine nuts, chopped

1 C Italian parsley, chopped

¼ C olive oil

¼ tsp salt

Sauté onion and carrot with a little olive oil in large kettle until tender. Add tomatoes with liquid, 2 C water, 1 tsp salt, and bring to a boil. Rinse and drain garbanzos and beans and add to kettle.

Cook for another 5 minutes until heated. In a separate bowl, mix the garlic, pine nuts, parsley, olive oil and ¼ tsp salt. Spoon chili into bowls and top with pesto sauce. Serves 4.

Nutrition Facts (1 serving = 1/4 recipe)

Calories 515, Fat 20 g, Saturated 3 g, Polyunsaturated 5 g, Monounsaturated 12 g, Trans fat 0 g, Cholesterol 0 mg, Sodium 1890 mg, Carbohydrate 66 g, **Dietary Fiber 13 g**, Protein 19 g, Vitamin A 57%, Vitamin C 41%, Calcium 18%, Iron 35%

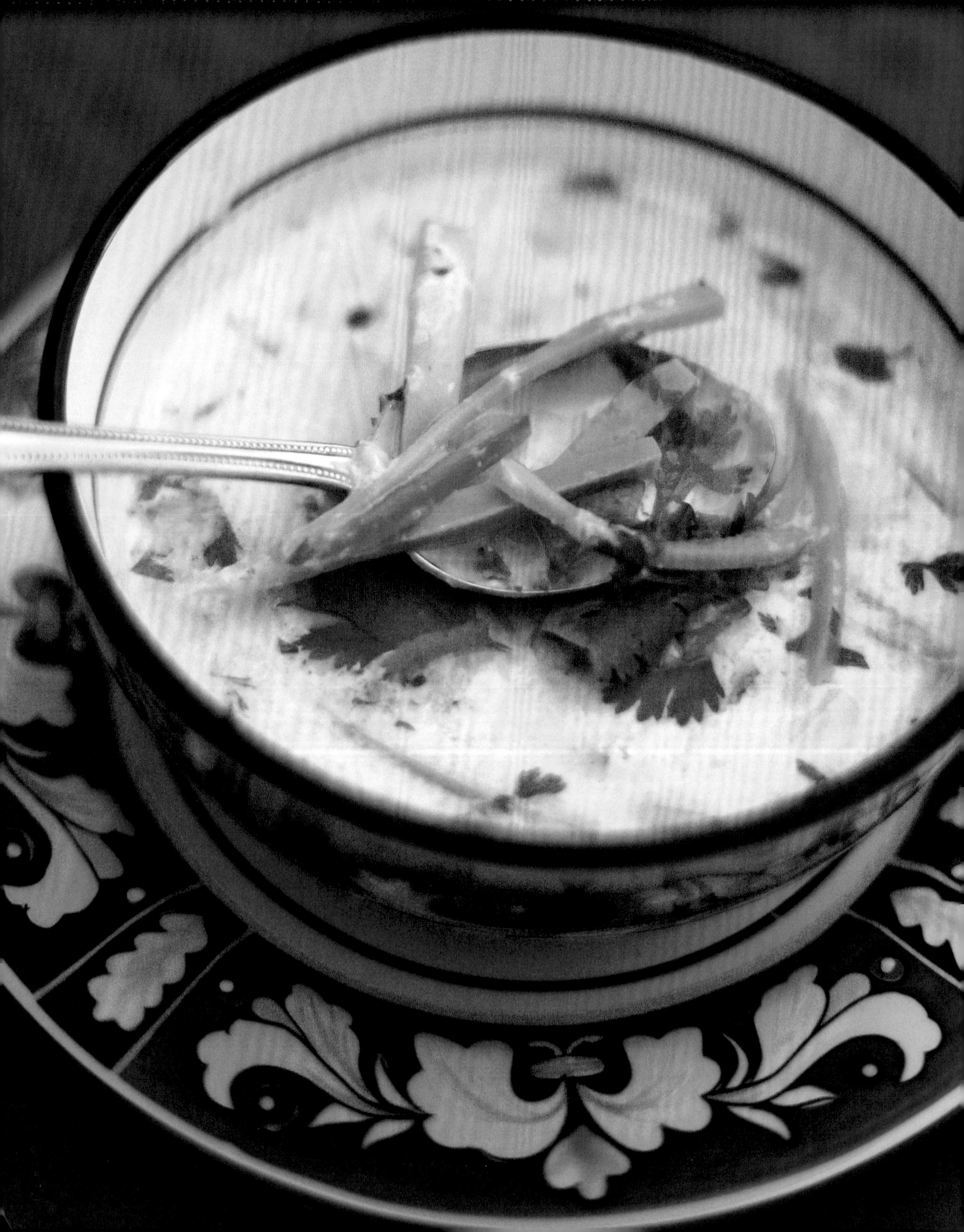

Tom Kah Soup

1 can light coconut milk

2 C water

1 Tbs fresh lime juice

1 - 2 medium carrots, sliced into thin strips

1 Tbs organic light soy sauce

2 tsp Thai seasoning

¼ tsp salt

1/3 bunch of cilantro, chopped

1/3 block of firm organic tofu, cubed

½ red bell pepper, sliced into thin strips

Put all ingredients into kettle and bring to a boil.
Cook for about 8 minutes or until carrots are cooked but still crisp.
Serves 4.

Thai seasoning can be found in the Asian section of the grocery store. The major ingredients are ginger, lemon grass, and garlic. If you can't find a Thai seasoning, use a mixture of those seasonings, and it will work.

Nutrition Facts (1 serving = 1/4 recipe)

Calories 153, Fat 12 g, Saturated 7 g,
Trans fat 0 g, Cholesterol 0 mg,
Sodium 498 mg, Carbohydrate 7 g,
Dietary fiber 2 g, Protein 6 g, Vitamin A 47%,
Vitamin C 30%, Calcium 24%, Iron 10%

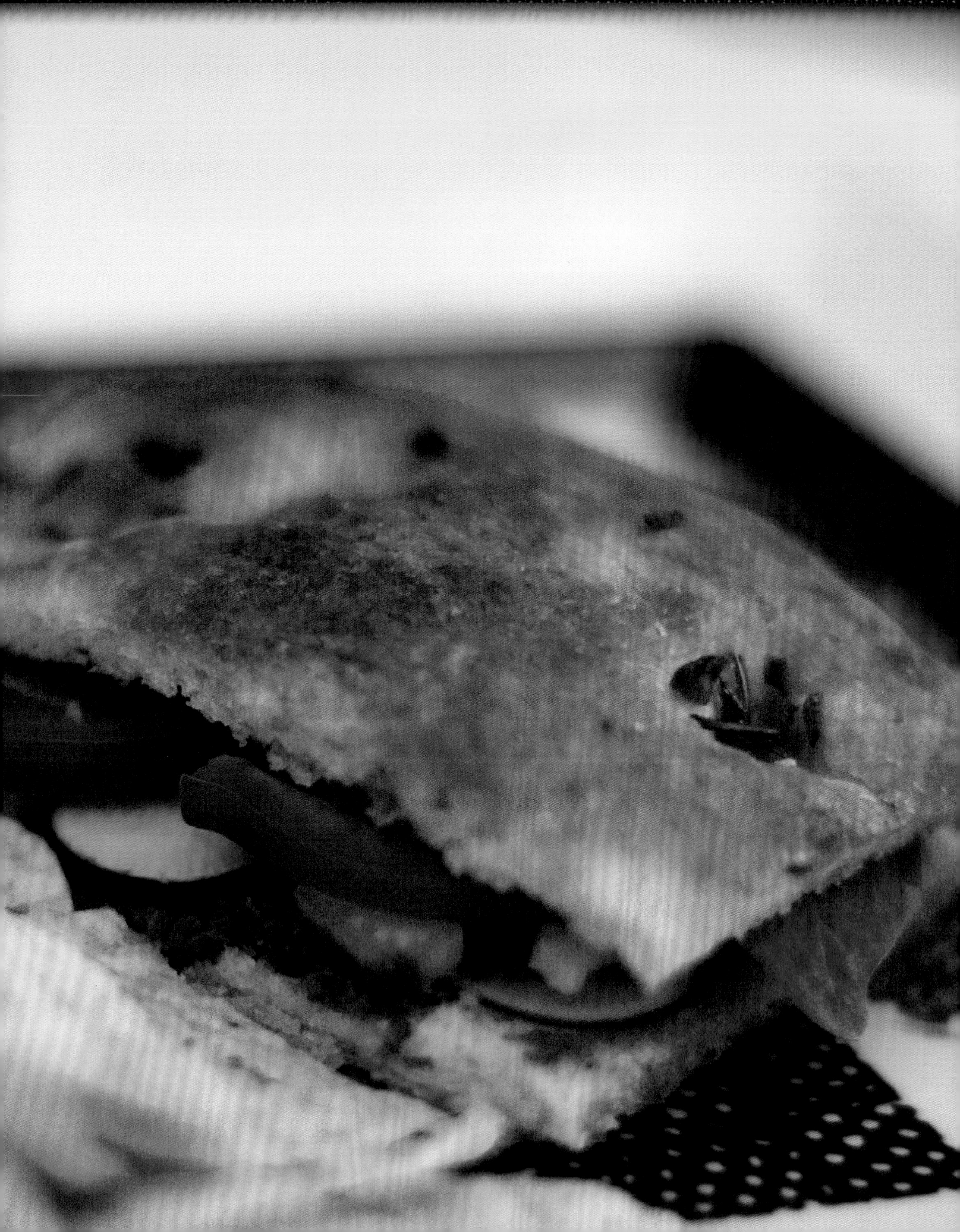

Karen's Veggie Sandwich

Sandwich

1 12-oz jar kalamata olives, pitted

1 cucumber, thinly sliced

1/2 - 1 stalk celery, thinly sliced

Fresh baby spinach leaves

1 loaf whole wheat French or foccacia bread

1 - 2 radishes, thinly sliced

1 red bell pepper, sliced into thin strips

Green onions, chopped

(Ideal bread is foccacia—it's a flat bread and won't need to be scooped out. French bread is quite thick, so that's why some of it will need to be scooped out.)

Dressing

½ C olive oil

2 tsp garlic powder

1 tsp oregano

1/3 C lemon juice

1 tsp salt

Slice loaf of bread horizontally. In food processor grind up the kalamata olives into an olive paste. Scoop out part of the lower half of the loaf of bread. Then spread the olive paste over the lower half the bread. Put cucumber slices on top of the olive spread and then layer the radishes, celery, and red pepper slices, and end with fresh baby spinach leaves. Mix dressing and pour over the inside top of loaf. You won't need the whole amount of the dressing. Place the top of loaf over the lower half and slice into 4 - 5 segments for sandwiches. This is one of our favorite sandwiches. Goes great with home-made soup.

Preparation Tip: If you want to make the sandwiches ahead the same day, wrap them in plastic wrap until ready to eat.

Nutrition Facts (1 serving = 1/5 recipe)

Calories 717, Fat 42 g, Saturated 4 g, Trans fat 0 g, Cholesterol 0 mg, Sodium 2172 mg, Carbohydrate 74 g, Dietary fiber 4 g, Protein 13 g, Vitamin A 30%, Vitamin C 76%, Calcium 7%, Iron 25%

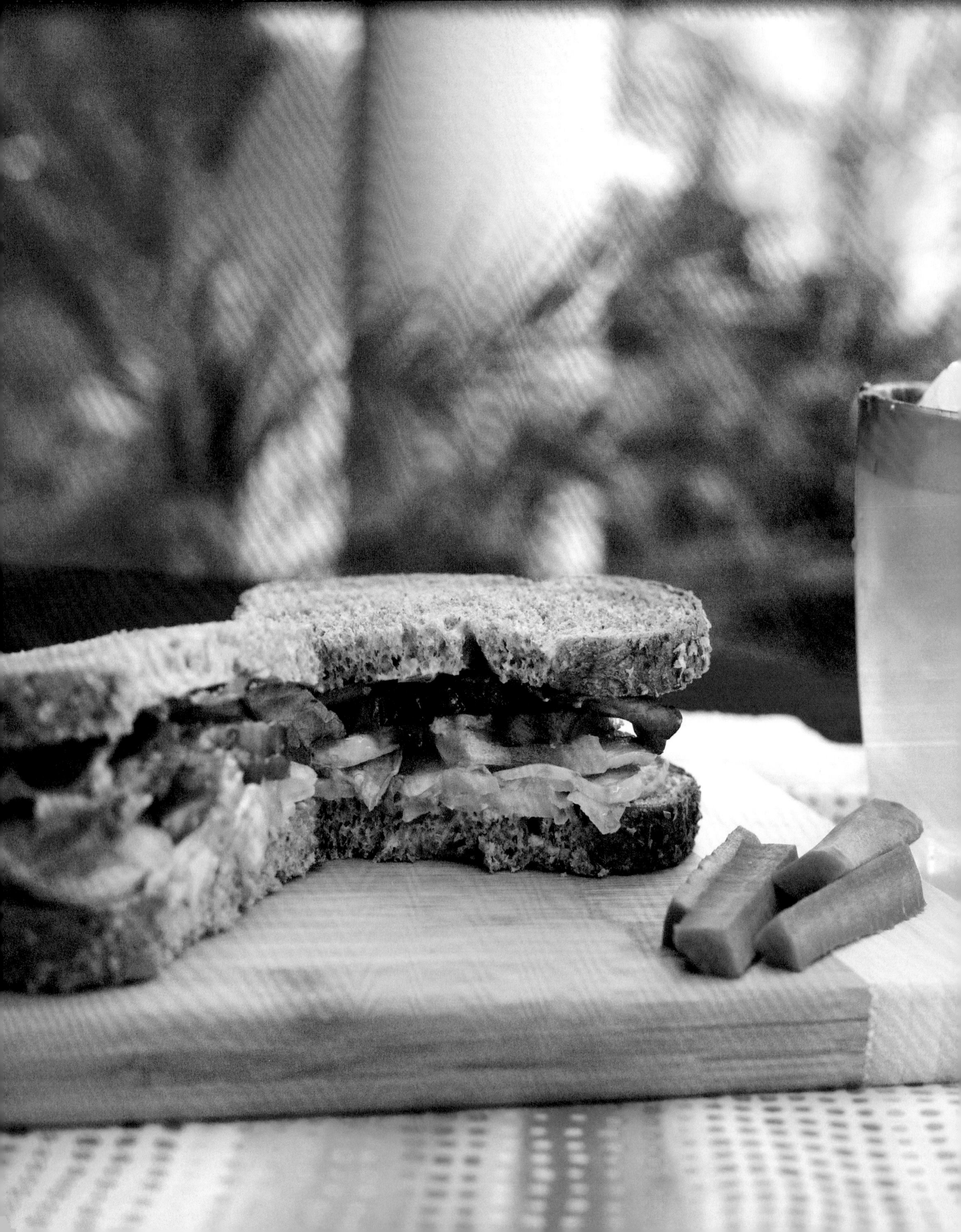

Garden Veggie Sandwich

1 - 2 summer squash, sautéed

Onion slices, sautéed

1 - 2 sliced tomatoes

Leaf lettuce

Vegenaise or mayo

Toasted whole grain bread slices

Sauté the summer squash and onions in olive oil. Slice tomatoes and any other veggie you may like to add. Spread Vegenaise on the toast and add veggies.

Hint: Pump the fiber and use Oroweat Double Fiber bread (6 gms fiber per slice).
The Double Fiber bread was counted in the Nutrition Facts.

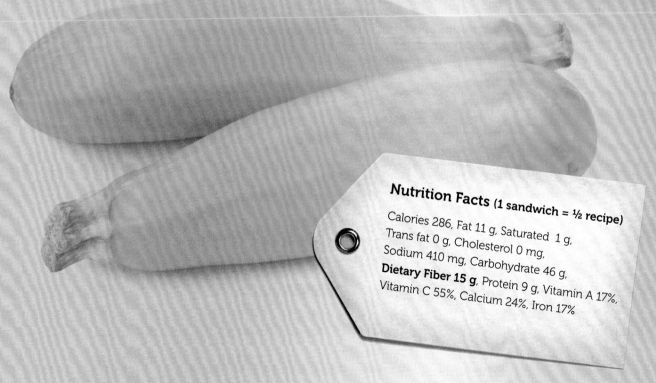

Nutrition Facts (1 sandwich = ½ recipe)

Calories 286, Fat 11 g, Saturated 1 g, Trans fat 0 g, Cholesterol 0 mg, Sodium 410 mg, Carbohydrate 46 g, **Dietary Fiber 15 g**, Protein 9 g, Vitamin A 17%, Vitamin C 55%, Calcium 24%, Iron 17%

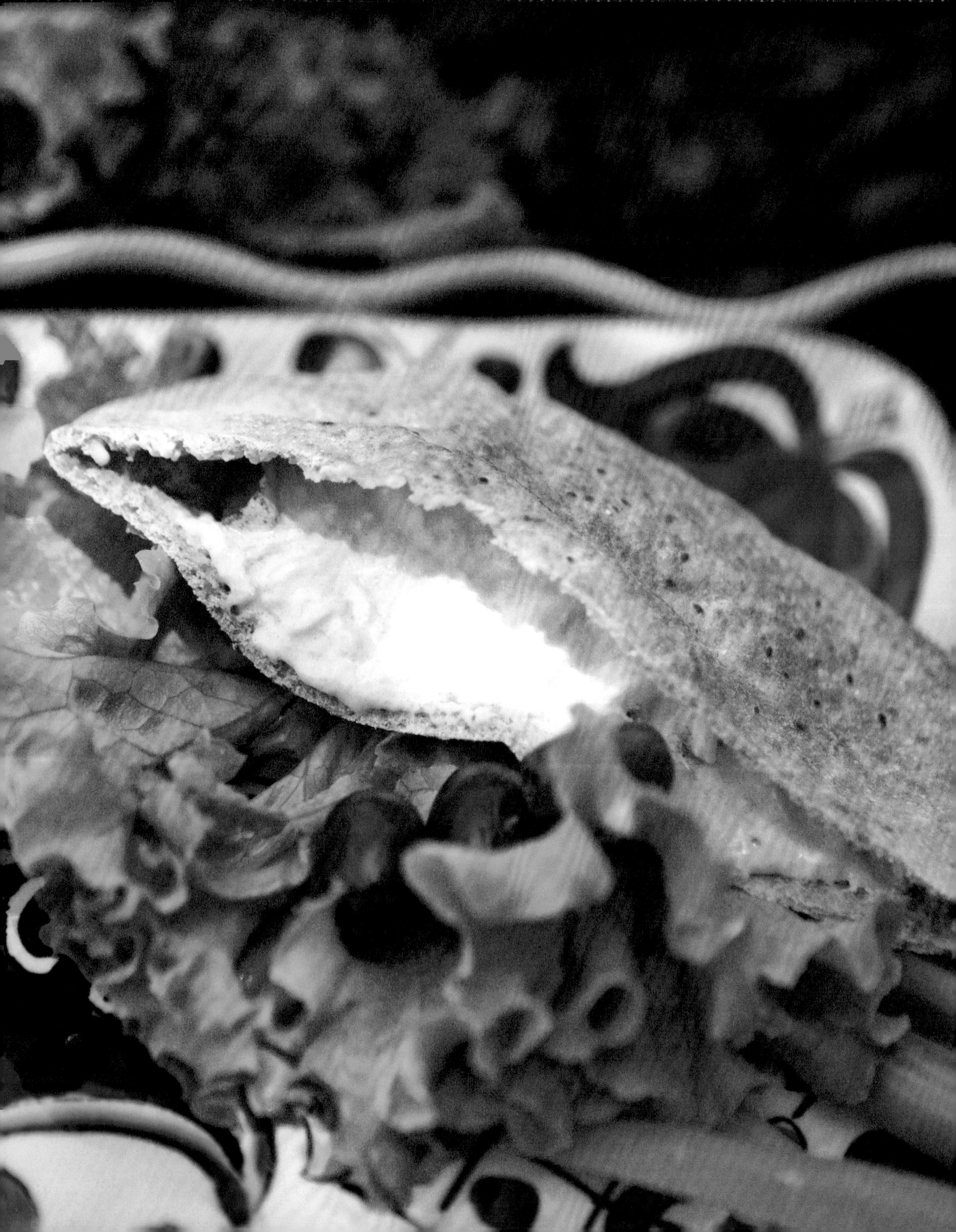

Pita Bread Sandwich

1 whole wheat pita pocket

2 - 3 Tbs hummus (p. 101)

1 tomato, chopped

2 Tbs chopped olives

1 green onion, chopped

½ avocado, diced

2 - 3 Tbs tzadzeki—also known as creamy cucumber sauce (p. 139)

Cut whole wheat pocket bread in half. Spread the hummus inside. Stuff the pocket with the chopped tomato, olives, green onion, and avocado. Top with tzadzeki.

Makes 2 sandwiches.

Hint: We like to use Lawry's seasoned salt or Tony's to sprinkle on the hummus.

Nutrition Facts (1 sandwich = 1/2 recipe)
Calories 338, Fat 24 g, Saturated 4 g,
Trans fat 0 g, Cholesterol 0 mg,
Sodium 321 mg, Carbohydrate 29 g,
Dietary fiber 6 g, Protein 6 g, Vitamin A 6%,
Vitamin C 19%, Calcium 4%, Iron 10%

Hummus

1 15-oz can garbonzos

1 clove garlic, minced

¼ C tahini (sesame seed butter)

3 Tbs lemon juice

1 tsp salt

1 - 2 Tbs fresh parsley, diced

Blend all ingredients in the blender. If it's too thick, add a little water and blend again.
Pour into a dish. I like to drizzle a little olive oil on top for flavor.

Nutrition Facts (1 serving = 1 Tbs)

Calories 26, Fat 1 g, Saturated 0 g,
Trans fat 0 g, Cholesterol 0 mg,
Sodium 119 mg, Carbohydrate 3 g,
Dietary fiber 1 g, Protein 1 g, Vitamin A 1%
Vitamin C 2%, Calcium 2 %, Iron 2%

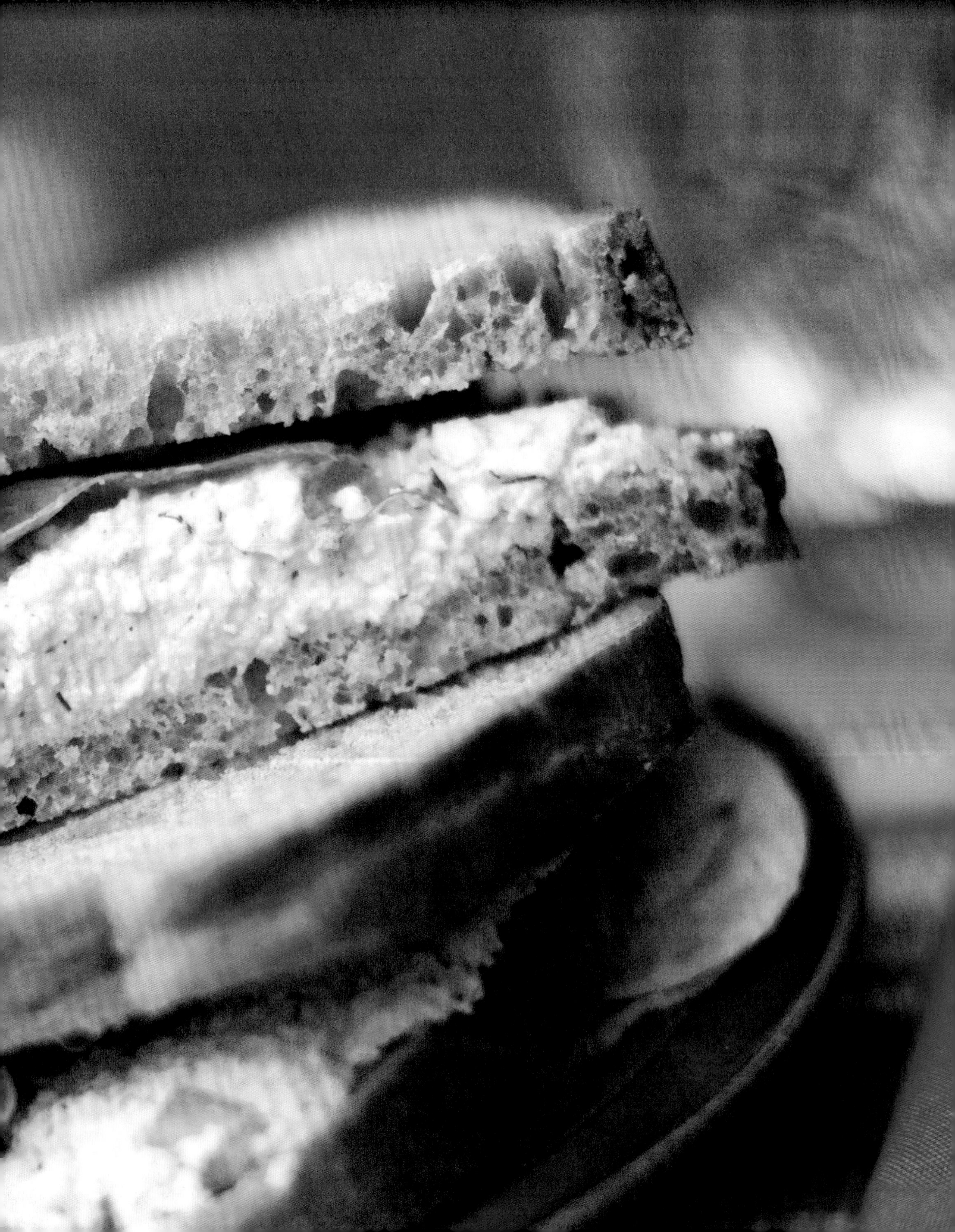

Tofu Egg Salad

1 pound firm organic tofu, drained

4 Tbs Vegenaise or mayo

Chopped celery

Chopped green onions

Chopped pickles

1 tsp turmeric

1 tsp dill weed

1/2 tsp salt (or to taste)

Nutrition Facts (1 serving = 1/6 recipe)

Calories 126, Protein 6 g, Fat 10 g, Carbohydrate 5 g, Dietary fiber 1 g, Calcium 136 mg, Iron 2 mg, Sodium 303 mg

Mash tofu with a fork. Mix ingredients together. Add chopped celery, green onions, and chopped dill pickles to mixture. Great on whole grain toast. Serves 6.

Hint: Adding veggies will boost the fiber, and if you use Oroweat Double Fiber bread, there are 12 gm of fiber in 2 slices.

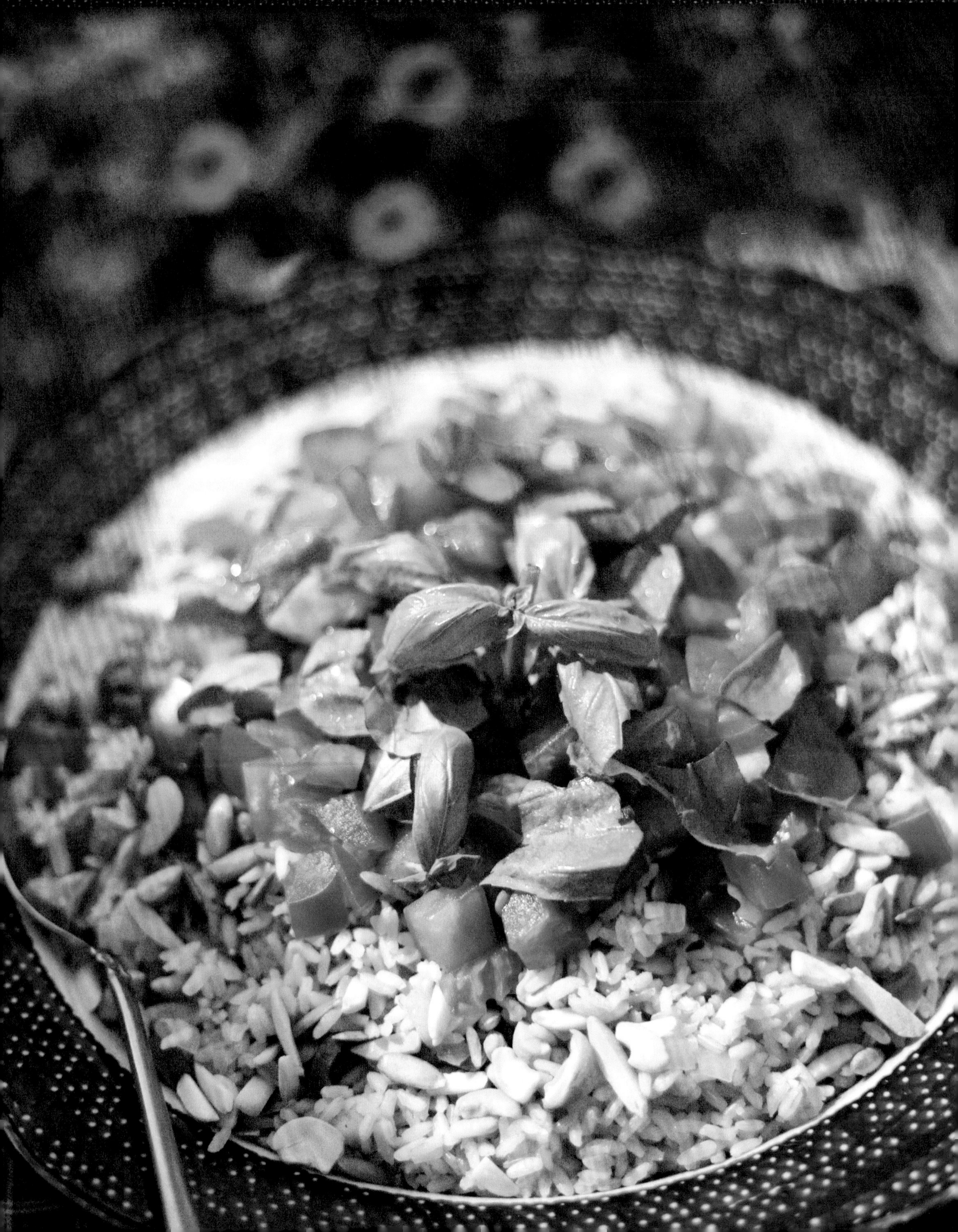

Crunchy Rice

8 C cooked jasmine brown rice

¾ C onions, chopped

¾ C celery, chopped

¾ C shiitake mushrooms, sliced

1 Tbs vegetarian chicken seasoning

1 tsp salt

2 - 3 tomatoes, chopped

(Optional: you can sprinkle a little cayenne in for flavor.)

When ready to serve, add:

1/3 C toasted cashews

1/3 C toasted slivered almonds

1/3 C toasted pumpkin seeds

1/3 C toasted sunflower seeds

Chopped fresh basil leaves

Cook the rice. After the rice is cooked, add the sautéed vegetables and chicken seasoning and salt. When you are ready to serve the rice, put the toasted nuts and seeds on top. Then add the chopped tomatoes on top and finally, sprinkle the chopped fresh basil leaves on top. Serves 8.

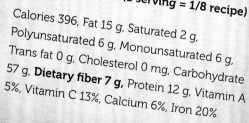

Nutrition Facts (1 serving = 1/8 recipe)

Calories 396, Fat 15 g, Saturated 2 g, Polyunsaturated 6 g, Monounsaturated 6 g, Trans fat 0 g, Cholesterol 0 mg, Carbohydrate 57 g, **Dietary fiber 7 g,** Protein 12 g, Vitamin A 5%, Vitamin C 13%, Calcium 6%, Iron 20%

A Taste of Thai

2 bunches asparagus, steamed

½ - 1 onion, cut and sautéed

1 firm water pak organic tofu, cubed

3 Tbs olive oil, 3 Tbs organic soy sauce

minced garlic, and salt to taste

In a frying pan, drizzle olive oil, and heat the oil to hot. Add the cubed tofu and fry until it's nicely browned. Then add the soy sauce and minced garlic and cook a little longer to season the tofu. Set it aside. (If you prefer to bake the tofu, you can drizzle 1 Tbs olive oil, 1 Tbs soy sauce, then add garlic and salt and mix gently in a bowl—then pour onto a baking sheet. Bake at 350° for about 20 minutes, until nicely browned.)

Thai Peanut Sauce

1 can light coconut milk

¾ C creamy peanut butter

½ tsp salt

1 - 2 Tbs fresh lemon juice

¼ C water

1/8 tsp red curry paste (optional)

1/3 C organic sugar or more to taste

Nutrition Facts, Fried (1 serving=1/5 recipe)
Calories 574, Fat 38 g, Saturated 11 g, Trans fat 0 g, Cholesterol 0 mg, Sodium 802 mg, Carbohydrate 40 g, **Dietary fiber 11 g**, Protein 25 g, Vitamin A 20%, Vitamin C 33%, Calcium 27%, Iron 60%

Nutrition Facts, Baked (1 serving=1/5 recipe)
Calories 523, Fat 33, Saturated 11 g, Trans fat 0 g, Cholesterol 0 mg, Sodium 562 mg, Carbohydrate 39 g, **Dietary fiber 11 g**, Protein 25 g, Vitamin A 20%, Vitamin C 33%, Calcium 27%, Iron 59%

Heat coconut milk in a kettle on low until it simmers. Then add peanut butter, sucanat, salt, and red curry paste. Simmer on low heat until sauce is well blended and begins to thicken.

Stir together steamed asparagus and sautéed onions. Put cooked brown rice on the plate, then asparagus, onions, and fried tofu. Top with peanut sauce and a sprinkle of unsalted, chopped peanuts.

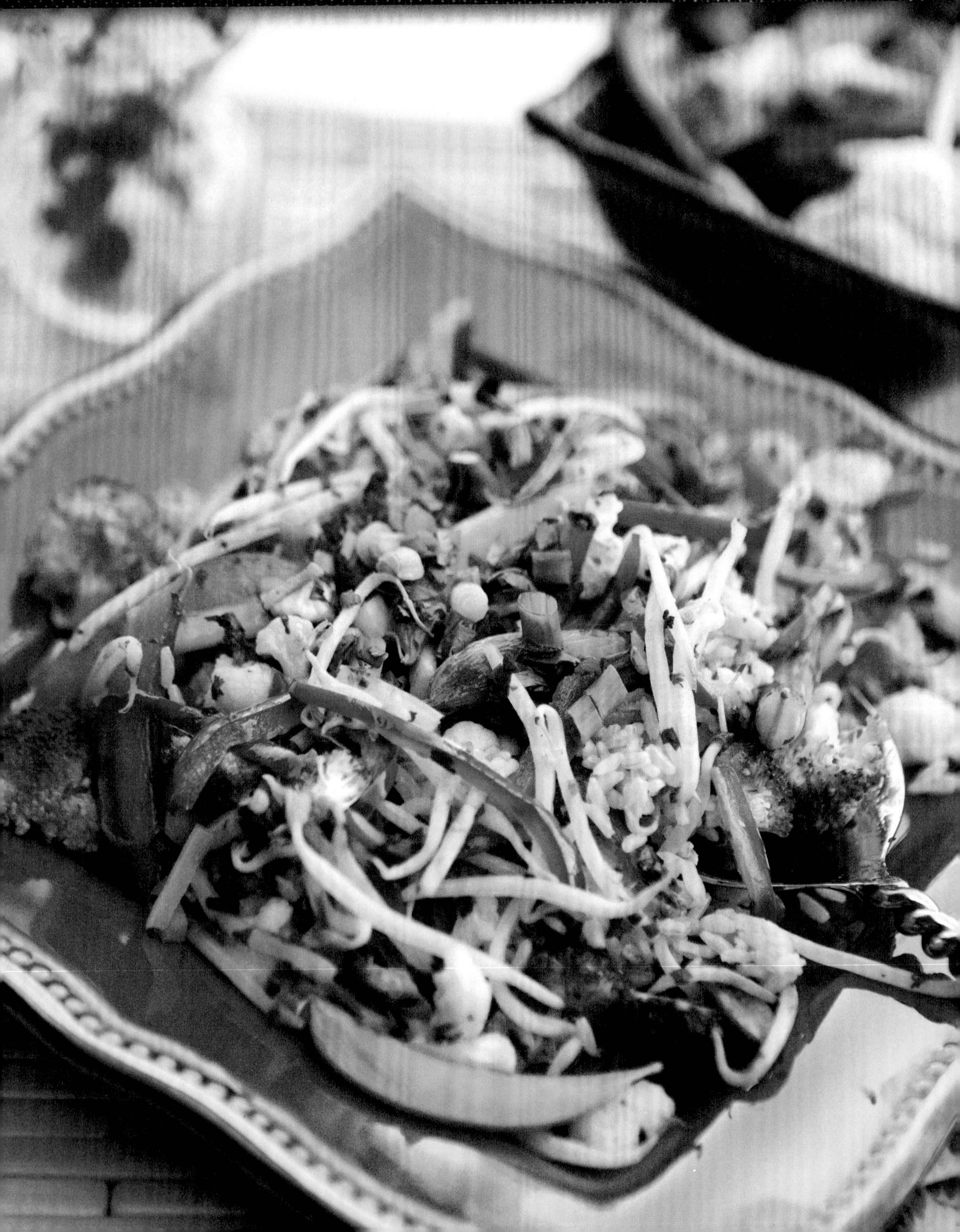

Broccoli Stir Fry

1 ½ C cauliflower florets

1 ½ C broccoli florets

1 ½ C pea pods

1 red bell pepper, sliced in thin strips

1 stalk celery, chopped

4 green onions, chopped

A handful of bean sprouts

½ bunch of cilantro, chopped

Olive oil

3 - 4 cloves of garlic minced

1 Tbs oregano

1 - 2 Tbs organic light soy sauce

Sauté fresh garlic and herbs in olive oil. Then add pepper, cauliflower, broccoli, pea pods, sprouts, and cilantro, in that order. Then add soy sauce. Serve this over jasmine brown rice. Serves 4 - 6.

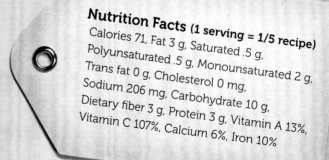

Nutrition Facts (1 serving = 1/5 recipe)
Calories 71, Fat 3 g, Saturated .5 g,
Polyunsaturated .5 g, Monounsaturated 2 g,
Trans fat 0 g, Cholesterol 0 mg,
Sodium 206 mg, Carbohydrate 10 g,
Dietary fiber 3 g, Protein 3 g, Vitamin A 13%,
Vitamin C 107%, Calcium 6%, Iron 10%

Butternut Squash Curry

1 butternut squash (med.)

½ Tbs crushed garlic

1 onion, chopped fine

Mrs. Dash & Mrs. Dash Italiano

1 Tbs Spike seasoning

1 vegetarian vegetable soup cube

1 large brown baking potato

1 C organic frozen corn

½ bunch cilantro, chopped fine

1 - 1 ½ tsp salt

2 small tomatoes, chopped

1 can coconut milk

Peel squash and cut in small chunks. Set aside. In kettle put 1 Tbs olive oil. Add garlic, chopped onion, 3 - 4 shakes each of Mrs. Dash & Mrs. Dash Italiano, 2 chopped tomatoes, Spike seasoning, and soup cube. Sauté. Next, add 4 C water and bring to a boil. Add squash and cook for about 30 minutes until slightly tender. Then add peeled and chopped potato. Add 1 can of coconut milk. Add 1 tsp salt. When potato is tender, add corn and chopped cilantro. Serve over brown rice. Serves 6.

Hint: This can also be a soup.

Note: Nutritional analysis was done with "Organic Gourmet Vegetable Bouillon." I like Organic Gourmet Vegetable Bouillon cubes the best.

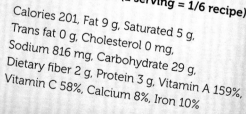

Nutrition Facts (1 serving = 1/6 recipe)

Calories 201, Fat 9 g, Saturated 5 g, Trans fat 0 g, Cholesterol 0 mg, Sodium 816 mg, Carbohydrate 29 g, Dietary fiber 2 g, Protein 3 g, Vitamin A 159%, Vitamin C 58%, Calcium 8%, Iron 10%

Chicken à La King

1 pkg frozen peas and carrots, cooked

½ C onion diced and sautéed

1/2 C sweet red pepper, diced and sautéed

Cashew Gravy

3 C water

½ C raw, washed cashews

½ C unbleached flour

Liquify the cashews and water in the blender until smooth.
Then add the flour to the blender and blend again.
Next, add to the cashew milk:

1 ½ tsp vegetarian chicken seasoning

¼ tsp garlic powder

½ tsp organic soy sauce or liquid aminos

1 ½ tsp salt

1 tsp onion powder

Nutrition Facts (1 serving = 1/9 recipe)
Calories 125, Fat 9 g, Saturated 1 g, Trans
fat 0 g, Cholesterol 0 mg, Sodium 21 mg,
Carbohydrate 10 g, Dietary fiber 3 g,
Protein 3 g, Vitamin A 3%, Vitamin C 72%,
Calcium 6%, Iron 8%

Cook mixture until thickened like gravy. Then add
the sautéed onions, sweet red pepper, and cooked
peas and carrots. Add diced tofu that's been sautéed (or baked) and slightly
browned, or 1 can diced Worthington FriChik. (FriChik is a soy meat substitute and can be
purchased at health food stores.) Serves 8.

Serving Tip: Pour chicken gravy over cooked brown rice or baked Pepperidge Farm pastry shells.
Also good over whole grain toast.

Vegetarian Goulash

1 ½ C large elbow macaroni

1 C onions, chopped

½ C fresh mushrooms, sliced (optional)

¼ C green bell peppers, diced

3 med garlic cloves, minced

1 Tbs olive oil

1 C frozen vegan burger crumbles

1 tsp Bill's Best or McKay's Beef Seasoning

2 14.5-oz cans stewed tomatoes

1 tsp basil

Cook macaroni in salted water until tender. Drain and rinse well. While macaroni is cooking, sauté vegetables in oil until soft. Add burger crumbles, cover with beef-style seasoning and brown mixture slightly. Add tomatoes and basil, cover, and simmer about 5 minutes. Stir in cooked macaroni and simmer until heated through. This recipe is from the Lifestyle Center of America.

Serves 2 - 3.

Hint: Using whole grain pasta will boost the fiber.
Another Hint: We use Morning Star Farms Meal Starters for the burger.

Nutrition Facts (1 serving = 1/3 recipe)

(Using "Grillers Recipe Crumbles" & "Bill's Best Vegetarian Beaf Seasoning")

Calories 377, Fat 7 g, Saturated 1 g, Trans fat 0 g, Cholesterol 0 mg, Sodium 762 mg, Carbohydrate 65 g, **Dietary fiber 7 g,** Protein 16 g, Vitamin A 11%, Vitamin C 61% Calcium 13%, Iron 37%

Eggplant & Garbanzo Ratatouille

4 cloves garlic, chopped

½ C onion, chopped

1 - 2 Tbs olive oil

½ tsp Italian seasoning

1 small eggplant, chopped

3 C fresh or canned diced tomatoes

¾ C canned garbonzos, rinsed and drained

½ C chopped fresh basil

Nutrition Facts (1 serving = ¼ recipe)

Calories 139, Fat 6 g, Saturated 1 g, Polyunsaturated 1 g, Monounsaturated 4 g, Trans fat 0 g, Cholesterol 0 mg, Sodium 143 mg, Carbohydrate 20 g, Dietary fiber 5 g, Protein 4 g, Vitamin A 10%, Vitamin C 30%, Calcium 5%, Iron 8%

Sauté the garlic, onion, and eggplant in the olive oil until tender. Add the seasoning, diced tomatoes, and garbanzos. Salt to taste. Pour over cooked brown rice, penne pasta, or a baked potato. Serves 4.

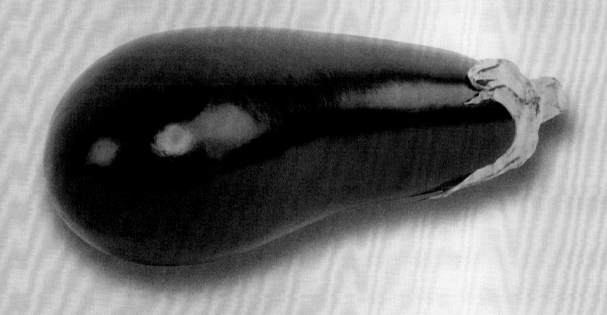

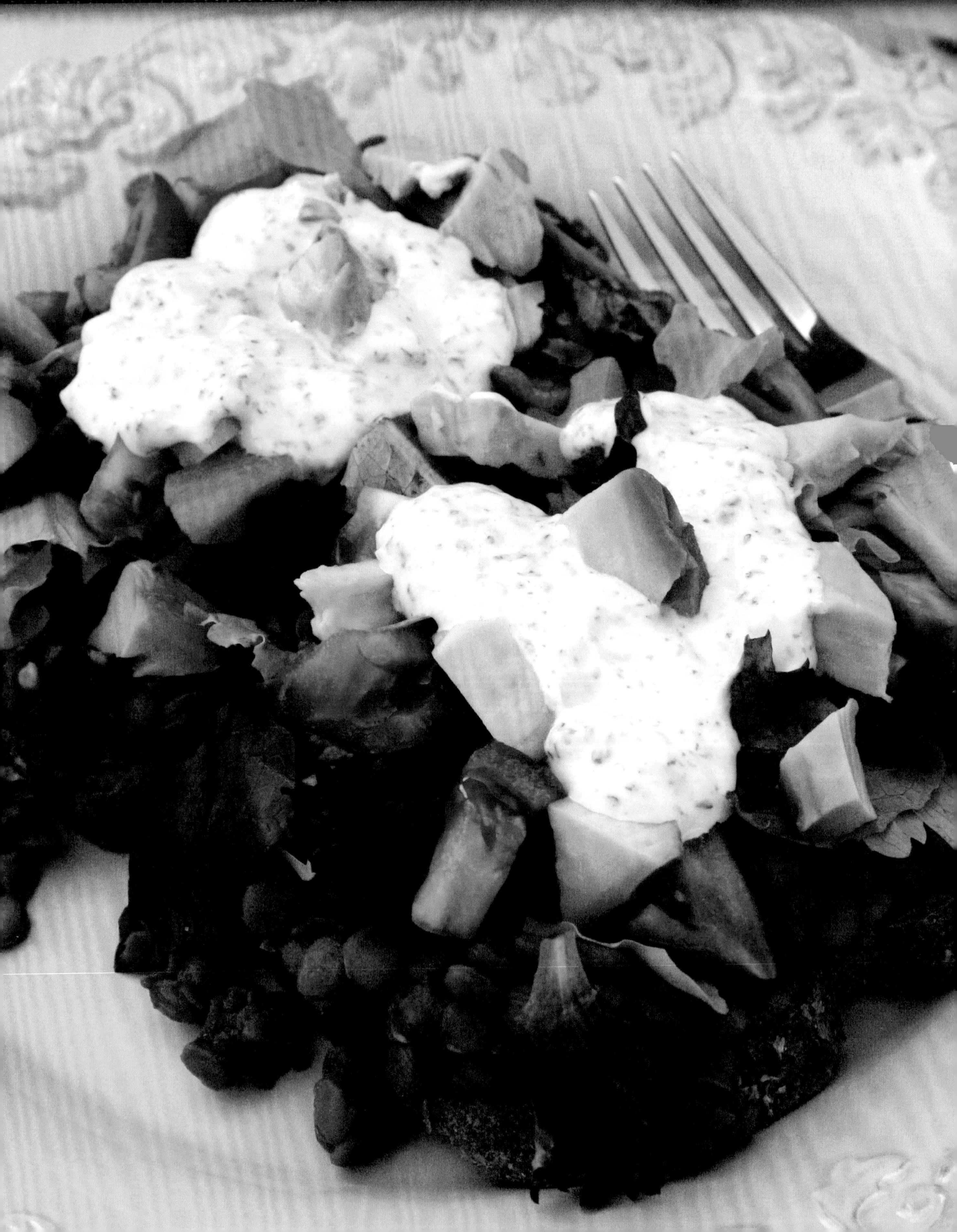

Lentil Haystacks

Lentils

2 C dry lentils

1 15-oz can tomato sauce

5 C water

½ C onion, chopped

1 ½ tsp salt

2 cloves minced garlic

I cook the lentils in the crock-pot overnight on low, but you can cook them on the stove top, as well. (Be sure to wash the lentils before you cook them.)

Haystack Toppings

2 tomatoes, chopped

1 C chopped olives (I like to mix black and natural green olives)

Green leaf lettuce, chopped

1 avocado, diced

½ C onion, chopped

Ranch dressing, salsa, or both

Whole grain toast

Nutrition Facts (1 serving = 1/6 recipe)

Calories 410, Fat 9 g, Saturated 1 g,
Trans fat 0 g, Cholesterol 0 mg,
Sodium 1354 mg, Carbohydrate 67 g,
Dietary Fiber 30 g, Protein 22 g,
Vitamin A 13%, Vitamin C 30%,
Calcium 17%, Iron 40%

Place the toast on your plate and top with cooked lentils.
Then add the chopped leaf lettuce, tomatoes, olives, onions,
and avocado. Top with your favorite topping. We like ranch dressing and salsa.

Hint: If you use Oroweat Double Fiber bread, it boosts your fiber count. We used it in the Nutrition Facts.

Veggie Fajitas

2 zucchini, sliced thin

2 summer squash, sliced thin

1 red bell pepper, sliced in strips

1 yellow bell pepper, sliced in strips

1 orange bell pepper, sliced in strips

1 small onion, sliced

1 carrot, sliced in thin strips

½ pkg Morningstar Farms Meal Starters Chik'n Strips (optional)

1 - 2 Tbs olive oil

Whole wheat tortillas

½ C Vegenaise or mayo

1/3 C cilantro, chopped

¼ tsp garlic powder

Nutrition Facts (1 serving = ¼ recipe)
Calories 407, Fat 27 g, Saturated 2g, Trans fat 0 g, Cholesterol 0 mg, Sodium 479 mg, Carbohydrate 39 g, **Dietary fiber 17 g**, Protein 13 g, Vitamin A 43%, Vitamin C 327%, Calcium 11%, Iron 14%. (When you use the La Tortilla Soft Wraps, you really boost the fiber, as their wraps have 12 - 13 gm of fiber in one wrap.)

Sauté veggies in olive oil until tender. Mix the Vegenaise with the chopped cilantro and garlic powder. Spread the Vegenaise mixture on a whole wheat tortilla, top with the sautéed veggies, and season with salt, Spike, Mrs. Dash, or Frontier Mexican seasoning to taste. Serves 4. (You can use other veggies in these, as well.)

Home-made Gluten Steaks

Gluten Steaks

1 ½ C Do-Pep (vital wheat gluten flour)

1 ½ C water

1 ½ Tbs flour

Put Do-Pep and flour in bowl; then add water. Mix. Set aside for ½ hour. Take gluten out of the bowl and slice and shape into cutlets. Drop slices of gluten into boiling broth. Simmer for one hour.

Dip gluten slices in a mixture of flour with nutritional yeast flakes or flour with Lawry's seasoned salt.

Fry in small amount of oil. Gluten may be frozen, thawed later, and then fried. A doubled recipe of this makes about 35 patties.

Serve gluten with mushroom gravy or a barbecue sauce.

Broth for Broiling

5 C water

3 Tbs Bill's Best or McKay's chicken or beef seasoning

½ C onion, chopped

1 Tbs celery salt or ½ C celery, chopped, with ½ tsp salt

1 Tbs Vegex or Savorex (health food store)

Hint: When I double the batch, I use 3 Tbs of the chicken seasoning and 3 Tbs of the beef seasoning.

Nutrition Facts (1 serving = 1 patty)

Calories 83, Fat 3 g, Saturated 0.5 g, Polyunsaturated 0.5 g, Monounsaturated 2 g, Trans fat 0 g, Cholesterol 0 mg, Sodium 4 mg, Carbohydrate 5 g, Dietary fiber 0 g, Protein 8 g, Vitamin A 0%, Vitamin C 0%, Calcium 2%, Iron 5%

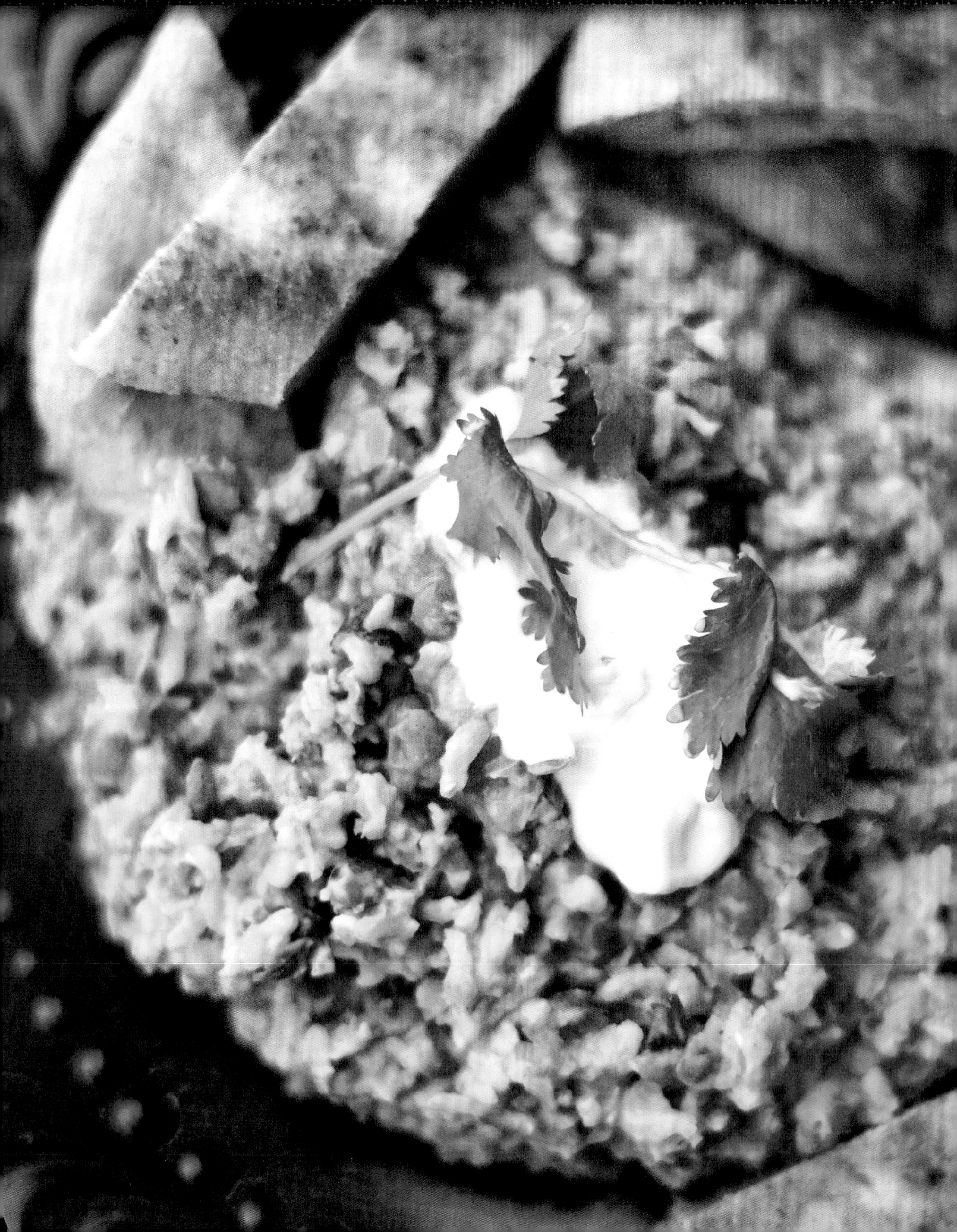

Indian Lentils & Rice

1 Tbs olive oil

1 C onion, thinly sliced

1 C uncooked jasmine brown rice

1 Tbs curry powder

1 ½ tsp salt

4 C water

1 C lentils

1 C fresh cilantro, chopped

½ C Follow Your Heart sour cream

Sauté onions in olive oil in kettle. Add rice, curry powder, and salt, and sauté for 1 minute. Add water and lentils and bring to a boil.

Cover, reduce heat, and simmer for 1 hour. Remove from heat and add cilantro and Follow Your Heart sour cream. This is good with naan (Indian bread), and a salad. Serves 3 - 4.

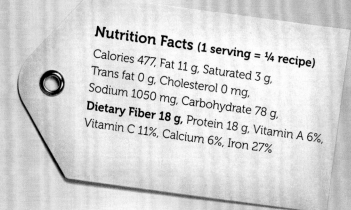

Nutrition Facts (1 serving = ¼ recipe)
Calories 477, Fat 11 g, Saturated 3 g,
Trans fat 0 g, Cholesterol 0 mg,
Sodium 1050 mg, Carbohydrate 78 g,
Dietary Fiber 18 g, Protein 18 g, Vitamin A 6%,
Vitamin C 11%, Calcium 6%, Iron 27%

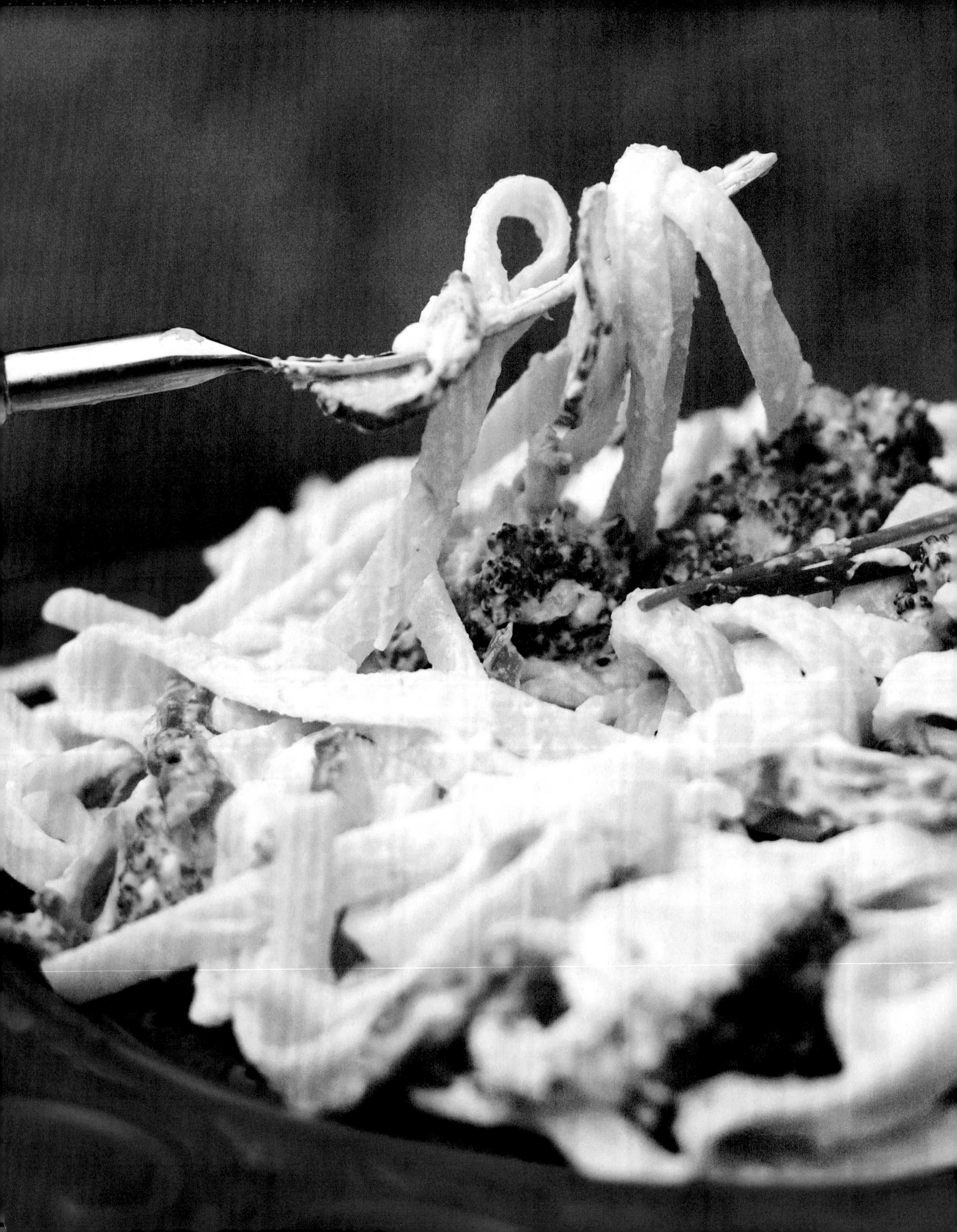

Pasta Primavera

Pasta & Vegetables

Cooked linguine pasta

1 summer squash, sliced

1 - 2 zucchini, sliced

½ C onions, sliced

1 C broccoli florets

1 red bell pepper, sliced into thin strips

½ C mushrooms, sliced (optional)

1 - 2 Tbs olive oil

Cook pasta according to directions on the box. While pasta is cooking, pour olive oil in another pan and add vegetables. Sauté for about 10 minutes until they are tender crisp. Add to cooked pasta. Then add the alfredo sauce to the linguine with vegetables.

Alfredo Sauce

½ C raw cashews

1 Tbs unbleached flour

¼ tsp onion powder

1 tsp basil

1 ¼ C water

1 Tbs chicken style seasoning

½ tsp salt

Pour cashews, flour, seasoning, onion powder, salt, and water into blender and blend well. Pour mixture into kettle and cook until thickened. Add basil and pour over linguine noodles. Alfredo sauce recipe is from *The Best of Silver Hills Cookbook*.

Serves 7.

Hint: Boost your fiber with whole- or multi-grain pasta.

Nutrition Facts (1 serving = 1/7 recipe)

Calories 294, Fat 8 g, Saturated 1 g, Trans fat 0 g, Cholesterol 0 mg, Sodium 373 mg, Carbohydrate 49 g, **Dietary Fiber 7 g,** Protein 10 g, Vitamin A 10%, Vitamin C 59%, Calcium 4%, Iron 14% (Recipe analyzed using whole grain linguine.)

Lentil Roast

1 ½ C cooked lentils

1 C organic soymilk

¼ C extra light olive oil

½ C onion, chopped

½ C pecan meal

1 tsp garlic powder

1 ½ C organic cornflakes

Salt to taste

Mix and put in oiled casserole dish. Bake at 350° for 45 minutes. Roast can be topped with ketchup, gravy, or barbecue sauce—also good just plain. Serves 6.

Note: if you can't find pecan meal, just grind pecans up in a food processor or blender.

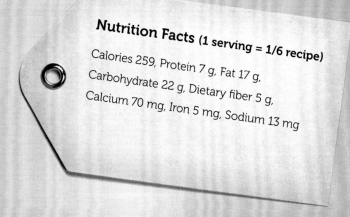

Nutrition Facts (1 serving = 1/6 recipe)

Calories 259, Protein 7 g, Fat 17 g,
Carbohydrate 22 g, Dietary fiber 5 g,
Calcium 70 mg, Iron 5 mg, Sodium 13 mg

Pecan Patties

5 home-made gluten steaks or Cedar Lake Hostess Cuts from the can

1 C whole wheat bread crumbs

1 C ground pecans

¼ - ½ C onion, chopped

½ tsp garlic powder

½ - 1 tsp salt

Ener-G Egg Replacer for 4 eggs

Optional: Use Daiya brand shredded cheese or non-dairy cheese of your choice, in small shreds, about ¼ cup.

In a food processor grind the pecans, then the bread, then the gluten. Add the ¼ C non-dairy cheese shreds. Chop the onion. Add the seasonings and mix well.
Take 1 - 2 Tbs of the mixture and shape into patties. You can fry them in olive oil. I fry the patties in extra virgin olive oil—it gives a great flavor to them.

These are some of our favorite patties. They are good with gravy, on a sandwich or with spaghetti and spaghetti sauce on top. Yield: 20 patties.

*Hint: The soy cheese really improves this recipe.
It helps to bind the patties together.*

*Another hint: If the pattie mix seems a little dry,
just add 1–2 Tbs of water to it.*

Nutrition Facts (1 patty)

Calories 68, Fat 5 g, Saturated 0 g, Tran fat 0 g, Cholesterol 0 mg, Sodium 93 mg, Carbohydrate 6 g, Dietary fiber 1 g, Protein 3 g, Vitamin A 2%, Vitamin C 3%, Calcium 3%, Iron 3%

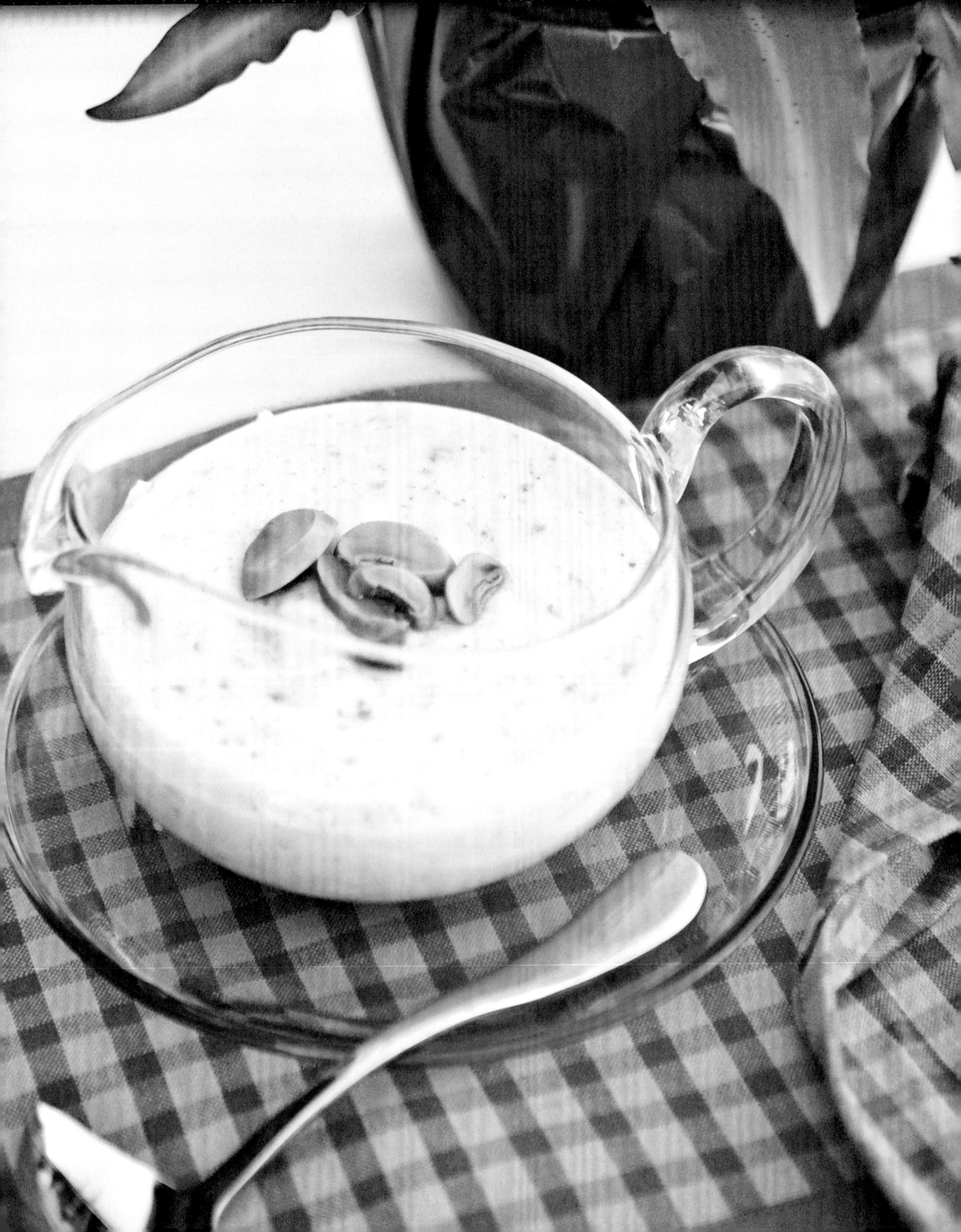

Mushroom Gravy

1/3 C canned mushrooms, with the juice

2 Tbs organic cornstarch

1 Tbs vegetarian beef seasoning

¾ tsp salt

2/3 C raw cashews

2 C water

Blend water and cashews until creamy. Add vegetarian beef seasoning, salt, and cornstarch and blend well. Add mushrooms and blend briefly. Pour the gravy into a kettle and cook until thickened. Stir frequently. Serves 6.

(Hint: always wash raw cashews first before using.)

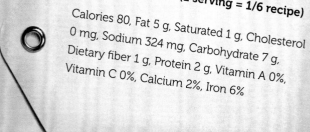

Nutrition Facts (1 serving = 1/6 recipe)

Calories 80, Fat 5 g, Saturated 1 g, Cholesterol 0 mg, Sodium 324 mg, Carbohydrate 7 g, Dietary fiber 1 g, Protein 2 g, Vitamin A 0%, Vitamin C 0%, Calcium 2%, Iron 6%

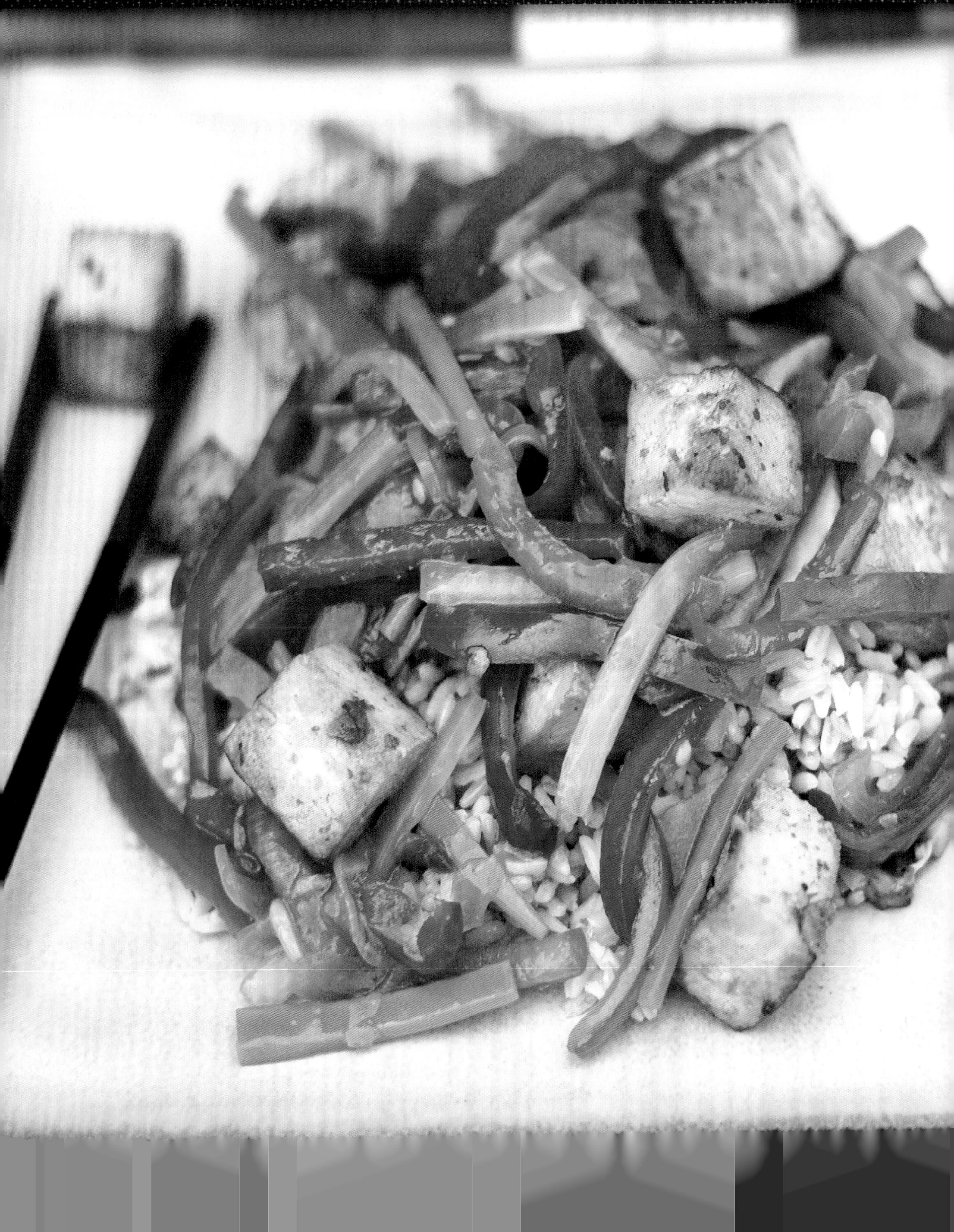

Simple Asian Stir Fry

4 mushrooms, sliced

1 red pepper, sliced

1 green pepper, sliced

1 stalk celery, sliced

1 carrot, sliced

½ onion, sliced

2 cloves garlic, minced

1 package organic tofu, cubed

5 Tbs olive oil

6 Tbs organic soy sauce

1 tsp organic cornstarch

4 oz water

Drain and cut tofu. Heat frying pan on high and fry tofu with 3 Tbs of olive oil, 3 Tbs of soy sauce, and garlic to season. Then stir fry vegetables in frying pan in 2 Tbs of olive oil. Add garlic, onions, carrots, bell peppers, celery, and mushrooms. Cook to desired tenderness. Season with 3 Tbs of soy sauce.

Mix 1 tsp of cornstarch with 4 oz of water. Add vegetables to tofu and cornstarch mixture. Cook to thicken a little. Serve hot over steamed brown jasmine rice.

Nutrition Facts (1 serving = ¼ recipe)

Calories 627, Fat 24 g, Saturated 3 g, Polyunsaturated 2 g, Monounsaturated 12 g, Trans fat 0 g, Cholesterol 0 mg, Sodium 935 mg, Potassium 331 mg, Carbohydrate 82 g, Dietary fiber 4 g, Sugars 4 g, Protein 21 g, Vitamin A 29%, Vitamin C 87%, Calcium 18%, Iron 14%

Spanakopita (Spinach Pie)

2 bags frozen chopped spinach

1 onion, chopped

½ tsp salt or to taste

3 - 4 tsp minced garlic

Olive oil

1 pkg fillo (sometimes also spelled "phyllo") dough

Tofu Cottage Cheese—½ recipe (p. 61.)

Sauté onion and garlic in a little water. Cook spinach, and while cooking, add the sautéed onion, garlic, and salt. Add tofu cottage cheese to spinach while it cooks.

In a 9 x 13 pan put 4 - 5 layers of fillo dough. Drain spinach. Put drained spinach mixture in pan on the fillo dough. Then put one layer of fillo dough on top of spinach. With a pastry brush, brush olive oil on the fillo dough. Put 5 - 6 layers of the fillo dough on the top, brushing each layer with the olive oil. Cut the spinach pie with a sharp knife into the size portions you want to serve. Then bake at 350° for 45 minutes. The fillo dough should be slightly browned and crispy. If you are going to eat it later, cover with aluminum foil and refrigerate. Then return to the oven without the foil and bake a little longer to get the fillo dough crispy before serving.

Top with Creamy Cucumber Sauce (p. 139).
Serves 8.

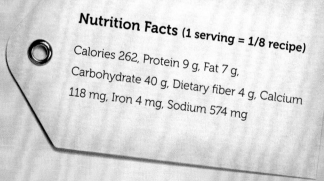

Nutrition Facts (1 serving = 1/8 recipe)

Calories 262, Protein 9 g, Fat 7 g, Carbohydrate 40 g, Dietary fiber 4 g, Calcium 118 mg, Iron 4 mg, Sodium 574 mg

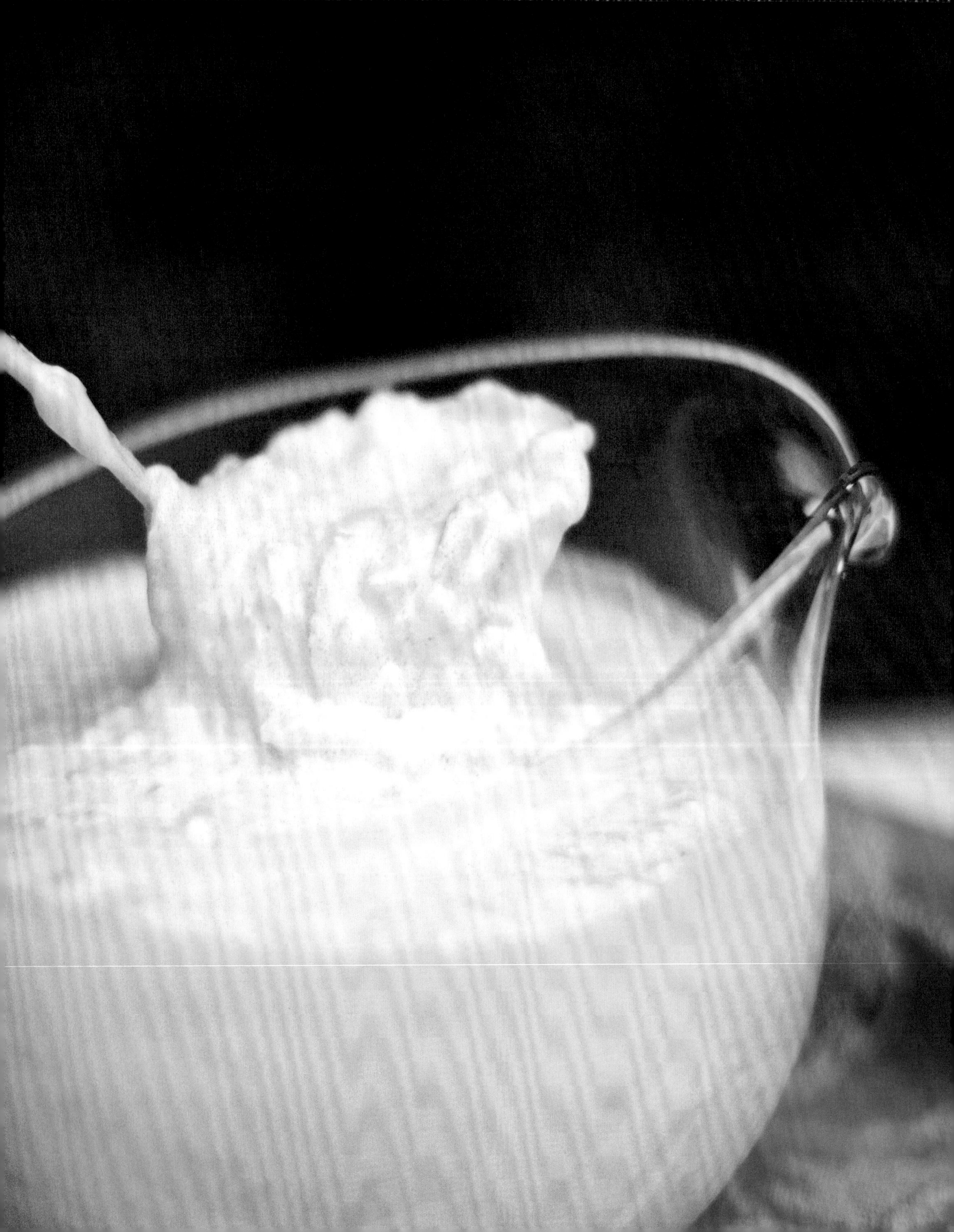

Creamy Cucumber Sauce

(Also known as tzadziki)

2 cucumbers, peeled and grated—drain well

3 - 4 garlic cloves, chopped fine or minced

¼ C fresh lemon juice

1 tsp salt

¼ C olive oil

1 tub Follow Your Heart sour cream

Mix together and use this to put on top of Spinach Pie (p. 137.) Pour on top after the individual serving is put on the plate. This also goes very well with pita bread sandwiches.

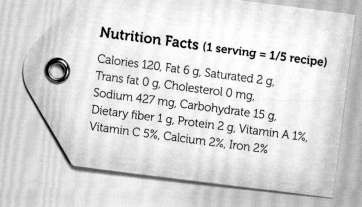

Nutrition Facts (1 serving = 1/5 recipe)

Calories 120, Fat 6 g, Saturated 2 g,
Trans fat 0 g, Cholesterol 0 mg,
Sodium 427 mg, Carbohydrate 15 g,
Dietary fiber 1 g, Protein 2 g, Vitamin A 1%,
Vitamin C 5%, Calcium 2%, Iron 2%

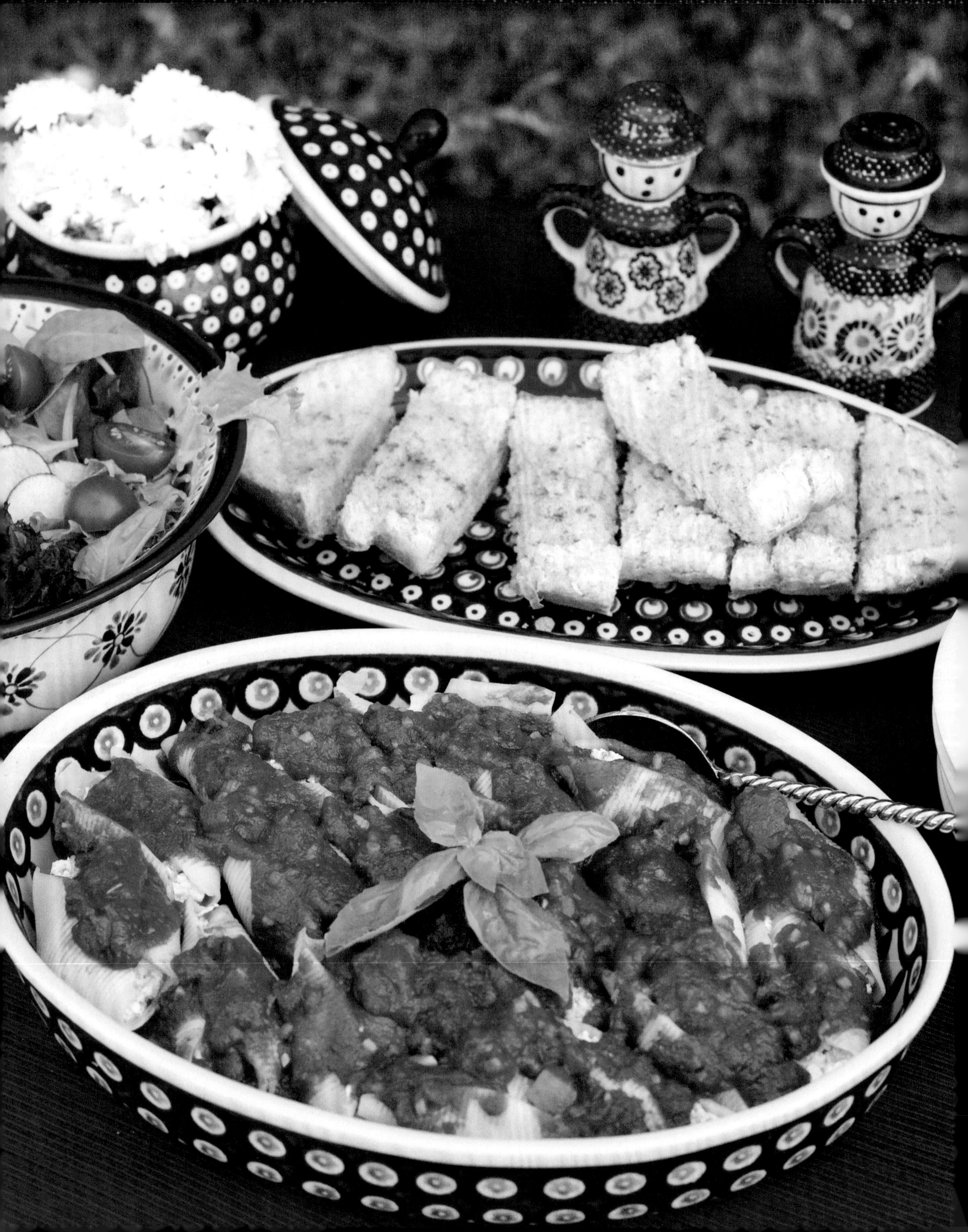

Stuffed Shells

Tofu Cottage Cheese

4 C organic tofu, extra firm, water packed

1 ½ tsp salt

2 ¼ tsp onion powder

½ tsp garlic salt

¾ C Follow Your Heart sour cream

2 Tbs chives

1/8 tsp citric acid or 1 - 2 Tbs lemon juice

Squeeze excess water out of tofu by pressing tofu block between hands. Crumble tofu in a bowl and add seasonings. Add citric acid to "sour cream." Stir into tofu mixture. Yield 4 C.

1 - 2 jars green and black olive spaghetti sauce

1 box jumbo shells

Cook jumbo shells. Spread a thin layer of spaghetti sauce in bottom of baking dish. Stuff cooled and rinsed shells with tofu cottage cheese. Place shells in baking dish. If the sauce is too chunky, you can blend it briefly. Pour over stuffed shells. Bake at 350° for 30 minutes. Makes 35 shells.

(Hint: If you don't have the green and black olive spaghetti sauce, just chop some olives and add to the sauce.)

Nutrition Facts (1 serving = 2 shells)

Calories 177 (calories from fat 51), Fat 6 g, Saturated 1 g, Cholesterol 0 mg, Sodium 688 mg, Carbohydrate 23 g, Dietary fiber 2 g, Sugars 3 g, Protein 8 g, Vitamin A 2%, Calcium 9%, Iron 8%

Sunflower Seed Loaf

1 ½ C whole wheat bread crumbs

1 large raw potato, shredded

1 1/3 C walnuts, ground

1 C sunflower seeds, ground

1 ½ C organic soymilk, or nut milk

2 cloves garlic, minced

½ C onion, chopped

1 ½ tsp salt

2 Tbs organic light soy sauce or Bragg's Liquid Aminos

½ tsp Frontier all purpose seasoning

Mix all ingredients together and put in an oiled dish and bake covered for 45 minutes at 350°. Uncover dish and bake 15 minutes longer. You can use gravy to go with this loaf if desired. Serves 6 - 8.

Nutrition Facts (1 serving = 1/7 recipe)

Calories 382, Fat 30 g, Saturated 2 g,
Trans fat 0 g, Cholesterol 0 mg,
Sodium 722 mg, Carbohydrate 28 g,
Dietary fiber 7 g, Protein 16 g, Vitamin A 3%,
Vitamin C 10%, Calcium 7%, Iron 21%

Vegetable Pot Pie

1 potato, cubed

2 carrots, sliced

¼ C onion, diced

1 stalk celery

½ C frozen lima beans

1 tsp salt

1 - 2 C diced "Heritage Chik'n Bites" or Worthington FriChik® (optional)

½ -1 recipe mushroom gravy (p. 133)

1 recipe single pie crust (p. 215)

Cook vegetables until almost tender in ¼ C water. Add Chik'n Bites and mushroom gravy. Pour gravy and vegetables into casserole dish. Top with pie crust. Bake at 425° for 30 minutes. Serves 8.

(8 servings includes gravy and crust)

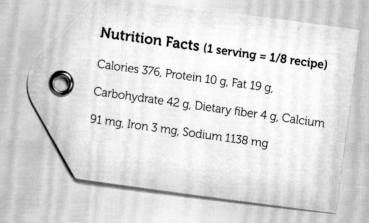

Nutrition Facts (1 serving = 1/8 recipe)

Calories 376, Protein 10 g, Fat 19 g, Carbohydrate 42 g, Dietary fiber 4 g, Calcium 91 mg, Iron 3 mg, Sodium 1138 mg

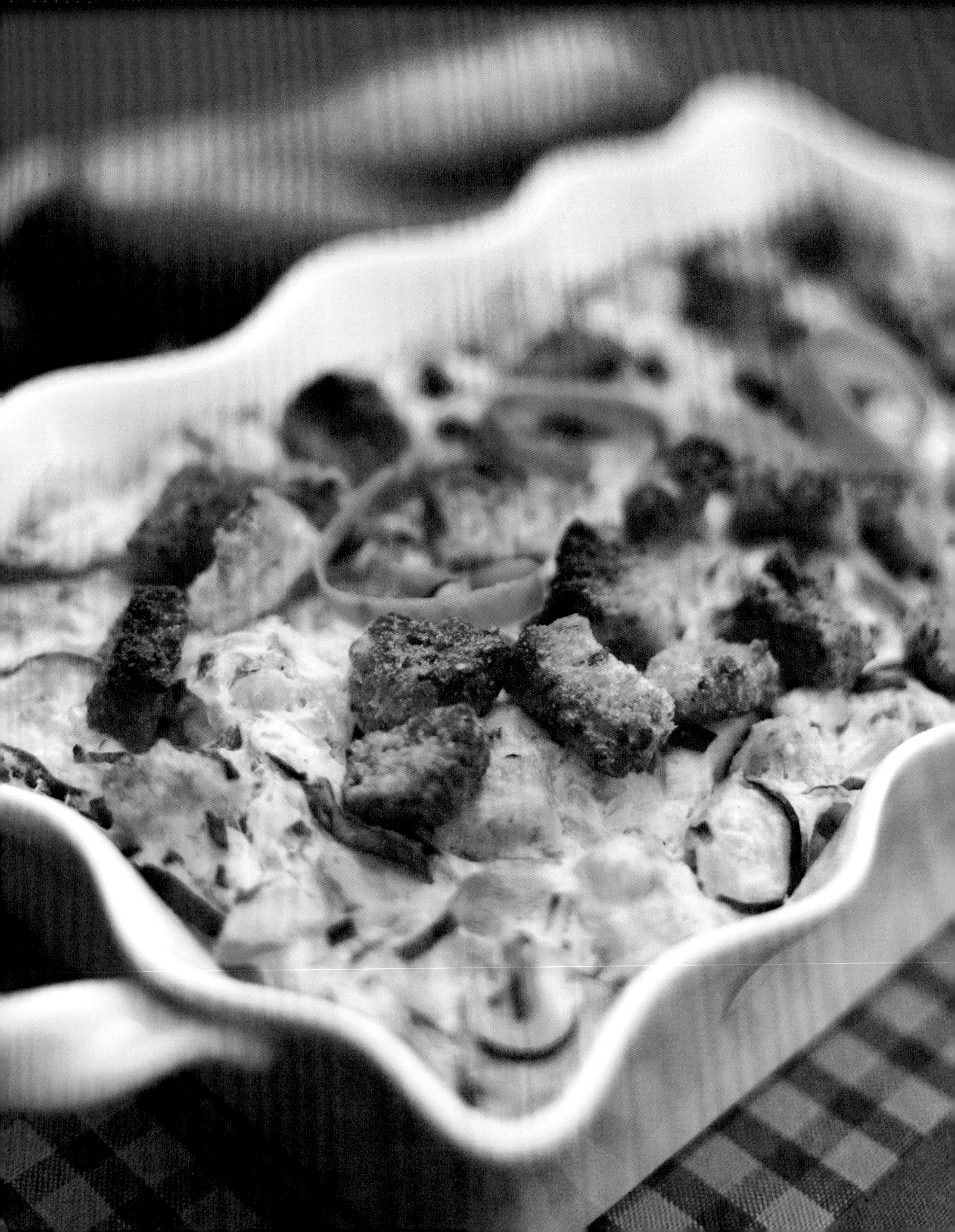

Zucchini Casserole

4 medium unpeeled zucchini, sliced

1 C carrots, shredded

½ C onion, chopped

2 ¼ C herbed croutons

½ recipe of Mushroom Gravy (p. 133)

½ C Follow Your Heart sour cream

1 - 2 Tbs olive oil

Cook zucchini and drain. Sauté the carrots and onion in olive oil. Stir in 1 ½ C herbed croutons, mushroom gravy, and sour cream. Stir in zucchini. Put in casserole dish and sprinkle the remaining croutons on top. Bake at 350° for 30 - 40 minutes. Serves 4. (The picture of this recipe is a doubled recipe.)

Hint: If you want to make your own croutons, toast 3 slices of whole wheat bread. Cut up toasted bread into cubes. Pour a little olive oil in a frying pan and add some all-purpose seasoning. Then add the bread cubes and toast them with the seasoning until crisp.

Nutrition Facts (1 serving = ¼ recipe)

Calories 344, Fat 18 g, Saturated 5 g,
Trans fat 0 g, Cholesterol 0 mg,
Sodium 721 mg, Carbohydrate 40 g,
Dietary fiber 5 g, Protein 8 g, Vitamin A 45%,
Vitamin C 49%, Calcium 8%, Iron 12%

Corn Tortillas With Veggies

4 organic corn tortillas

Fried gluten strips or Morningstar Farms Chik'n Strips

2 - 3 tomatoes, chopped

2 avocados, diced (optional)

1 bunch cilantro, chopped

1 small red onion, chopped

Heat corn tortillas. Fill tortillas with fried gluten, chopped tomatoes, chopped cilantro, chopped red onion, and chopped avocados, and cover with salsa.

Hint: You can use 6 Morningstar Farm Chik'n Strips cut in half for this, or your own gluten cut in strips—or you can even use baked or fried tofu cut in cubes. Very tasty.

Nutrition Facts (1 serving = ¼ recipe)
Calories 241, Fat 16 g, Saturated 2 g,
Trans fat 0 g, Cholesterol 0 mg,
Sodium 85 mg, Carbohydrate 23 g,
Dietary Fiber 9 g, Sugars 4 g, Protein 7 g,
Vitamin A 20%, Vitamin C 37%,
Calcium 5%, Iron 9%.
(Avocados included in the Nutrition Facts)

Roasted Cauliflower & Broccoli

4 - 5 C of broccoli, stems trimmed

4 - 5 C of cauliflower, stems trimmed

5 - 6 cloves of garlic, cut in long strips

Salt to taste

3 - 4 Tbs extra virgin olive oil

1 fresh lemon

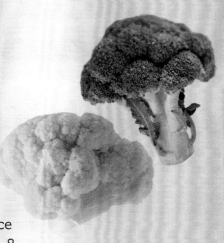

Wash vegetables and trim stems. Put veggies in a bowl and add garlic strips and salt, and drizzle olive oil on top. Mix veggies well and put on a cookie sheet and bake at 425° for 20 - 25 minutes until tender. After baking, squeeze the juice from a fresh lemon and drizzle over the vegetables. Serves 6 - 8.

Nutrition Facts (1 serving = 1/7 recipe)

Calories 91, Fat 7 g, Saturated 1 g,
Polyunsaturated 1 g, Monounsaturated 5 g,
Trans fat 0 g, Cholesterol 0 mg, Sodium 32 mg,
Carbohydrate 7 g, Dietary fiber 2 g, Protein 3 g,
Vitamin A 10%, Vitamin C 102%, Calcium 5%,
Iron 5%

Roasted Potatoes

8 large red potatoes

6 cloves garlic. minced

3 - 4 sprigs fresh rosemary

½ tsp salt

1 tsp Frontier all-purpose seasoning

1 tsp onion powder

1 - 2 Tbs olive oil or to taste

Vegenaise (optional)

Cut each potato into 8 wedges. Combine all ingredients and mix well. Bake at 450°
for 30 minutes until done. Top with a dollop of Vegenaise when serving. Serves 6 - 8.

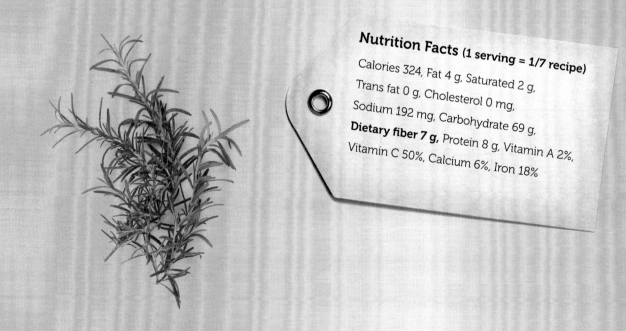

Nutrition Facts (1 serving = 1/7 recipe)
Calories 324, Fat 4 g, Saturated 2 g,
Trans fat 0 g, Cholesterol 0 mg,
Sodium 192 mg, Carbohydrate 69 g,
Dietary fiber 7 g, Protein 8 g, Vitamin A 2%,
Vitamin C 50%, Calcium 6%, Iron 18%

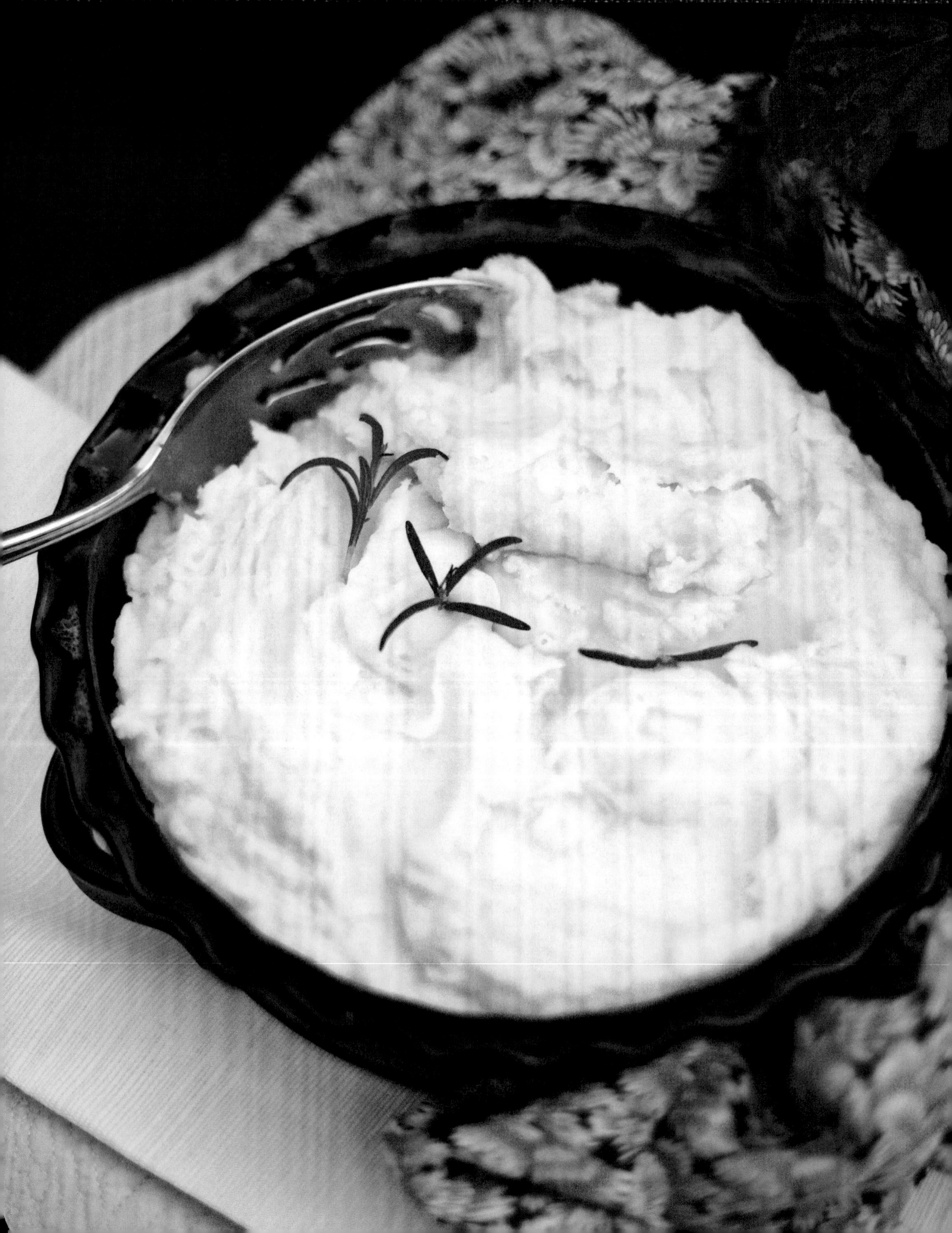

Whipped Potatoes

4 - 5 potatoes, peeled and cooked

Water from cooked potatoes

½ tub or more of Follow Your Heart sour cream

Salt to taste

Peel potatoes and cut into quarters. Cook in enough water to cover potatoes. Remove potatoes and put in a bowl. Add a little potato water, some Follow Your Heart sour cream, and salt. Mix with a potato masher or use an electric mixer and whip until smooth and fluffy. Add more sour cream as needed. When ready to serve, you can add 1 - 2 Tbs of Earth Balance margarine on top. These can be prepared the day ahead and refrigerated, then reheated. They are best though, the day you make them.

Nutrition Facts (1 serving = 1/5 recipe)

Calories 249, Fat 6 g, Saturated 3 g, Trans fat 0 g, Cholesterol 0 mg, Carbohydrate 44 g, Dietary fiber 4 g, Protein 5 g, Vitamin A 0%, Vitamin C 50%, Calcium 3%, Iron 9%

Roasted Asparagus

1 bunch asparagus

3 - 5 cloves garlic, crushed

1 - 2 Tbs olive oil

Salt to taste

1 ½ tsp fresh lemon juice

Trim off the tough ends of the asparagus. Cut asparagus into 1 in. sections (optional). Mix all ingredients together in a bowl. Spread on cookie sheet. Bake at 425° on top rack of oven 15 - 20 minutes, until slightly brown. Stir 2 - 3 times while baking. Pour lemon juice over asparagus after it's baked.

Nutrition Facts (1 serving = 1/5 recipe)

Calories 62, Fat 4 g, Saturated 1 g, Polyunsaturated 0 g, Monounsaturated 3 g, Trans fat 0 g, Cholesterol 0 mg, Sodium 2 mg, Potassium 205 mg, Carbohydrate 5 g, Dietary fiber 2 g, Sugars 2 g, Protein 2 g, Vitamin A 6%, Vitamin C 11%, Calcium 3%, Iron 12%

Popcorn

10 C of popped corn (air popped)

3 Tbs or more of extra light olive oil

2 - 3 Tbs of nutritional yeast flakes or to taste

Make popcorn sufficient to make about 10 C of popped corn in an air popper.
Drizzle extra light olive oil over the popped corn, salt to taste, and sprinkle nutritional yeast flakes over all. Very tasty.

(Hint: Nutritional yeast is a good source of B complex vitamins.)

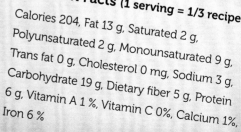

Nutrition Facts (1 serving = 1/3 recipe)

Calories 204, Fat 13 g, Saturated 2 g, Polyunsaturated 2 g, Monounsaturated 9 g, Trans fat 0 g, Cholesterol 0 mg, Sodium 3 g, Carbohydrate 19 g, Dietary fiber 5 g, Protein 6 g, Vitamin A 1 %, Vitamin C 0%, Calcium 1%, Iron 6 %

Salsa

1 sweet onion

¼ - ½ jalapeño pepper (optional)

1 bunch cilantro, stems removed

4 - 5 large tomatoes

Juice of 1 - 2 limes

½ tsp Lawry's salt or to taste

½ tsp garlic salt or to taste

Pulse all ingredients in a food processor so the salsa is still chunky.

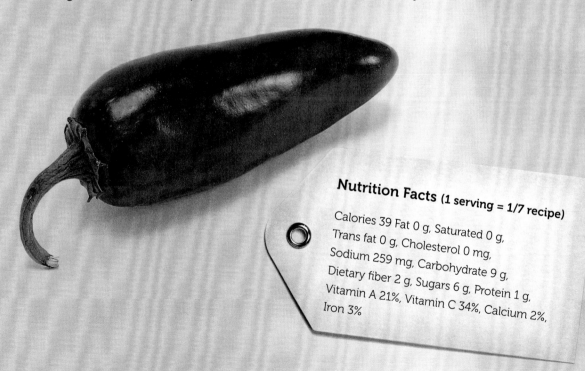

Nutrition Facts (1 serving = 1/7 recipe)

Calories 39 Fat 0 g, Saturated 0 g,
Trans fat 0 g, Cholesterol 0 mg,
Sodium 259 mg, Carbohydrate 9 g,
Dietary fiber 2 g, Sugars 6 g, Protein 1 g,
Vitamin A 21%, Vitamin C 34%, Calcium 2%,
Iron 3%

Pesto Pizza

Pesto Sauce for One Pizza

½ C toasted pine nuts or walnuts

1 - 2 cloves of garlic, crushed

2 C fresh basil

1/3 C extra virgin olive oil

½ tsp salt

Blend all ingredients in the blender. You can use this on pizza, with pasta, or on a sandwich. Serves 4 - 6. Nutrition Facts for sauce: Serving size = 1 serving, servings per recipe 5, calories 240, calories from fat 219, fat 24 g, saturated 3 g, cholesterol 0 mg, sodium 221 mg, carbohydrate 3 g, dietary fiber 1 g, protein 5 g, Vitamin A 4%, Vitamin C 4%, Calcium 2%, Iron 11%.

Pizza Crust Made in Bread Machine—Makes 2 Crusts

1 1/3 C whole wheat flour

1 1/3 C unbleached flour

2 Tbs vital wheat gluten

1 tsp salt

1 ½ tsp Italian seasoning

2 Tbs honey

2 Tbs olive oil

1 C warm water

1 ½ tsp yeast

Mix dry ingredients. In bread machine put the honey, olive oil, warm water and then add the flour mixture. Even the flour out and make a well in the center and add the yeast. Close the lid and set machine on the dough cycle. This makes 2 crusts. When the cycle is finished take enough dough to make one crust and you can freeze the rest of it. Spread the dough on the pizza pan, poke the center of the crust with a fork in several places so it won't puff up and then bake just the crust for 10–15 minutes at 375 degrees until the crust starts to brown. Then take it out of the oven, spread the pesto sauce on the crust. Top with sliced tomatoes, sliced green olives, sliced black olives, sliced artichoke hearts, chopped onions and then you can sprinkle Parmazaan (optional) on top. Return the pizza to the oven for 10–15 minutes or until done.

Nutrition Facts (1 slice = 1/16 recipe)

Calories 98, Fat 2 g, Saturated 0 g, Trans fat 0 g, Cholesterol 0 mg, Sodium 147 mg, Carbohydrate 18 g, Dietary fiber 2 g, Protein 3 g, Vitamin A 1%, Vitamin C 1%, Calcium 1%, Iron 6%

Three-Grain Bread

(For Bread Machines)

2 C white wheat flour

1/3 C rye flour, white or medium

1/3 C rolled oats

2 Tbs vital wheat gluten

1 tsp salt

2 Tbs olive oil

2 Tbs honey

1 C warm water

1 ½ tsp yeast

Mix the flours, oats, gluten, and salt. In the bread machine, put the olive oil, honey, and warm water. Add the flour mixture, even it out, and make a little well in the center. Put the yeast in the well and close the lid. Put the bread machine on the dough cycle. When the cycle is finished (about 1 ½ hours later), take the dough out and roll and shape it into a loaf. Put the loaf into an oiled bread pan. Have the oven preheated to 200° for about 5 minutes. Turn the oven off and put the loaf in the oven for 30 minutes to rise. After the 30 minutes, turn the oven temperature to 350° and bake for 40 - 45 minutes. Remove bread from pan and place on a wire rack to cool.

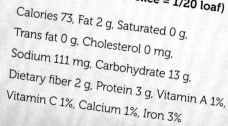

Nutrition Facts (1 slice = 1/20 loaf)

Calories 73, Fat 2 g, Saturated 0 g,
Trans fat 0 g, Cholesterol 0 mg,
Sodium 111 mg, Carbohydrate 13 g,
Dietary fiber 2 g, Protein 3 g, Vitamin A 1%,
Vitamin C 1%, Calcium 1%, Iron 3%

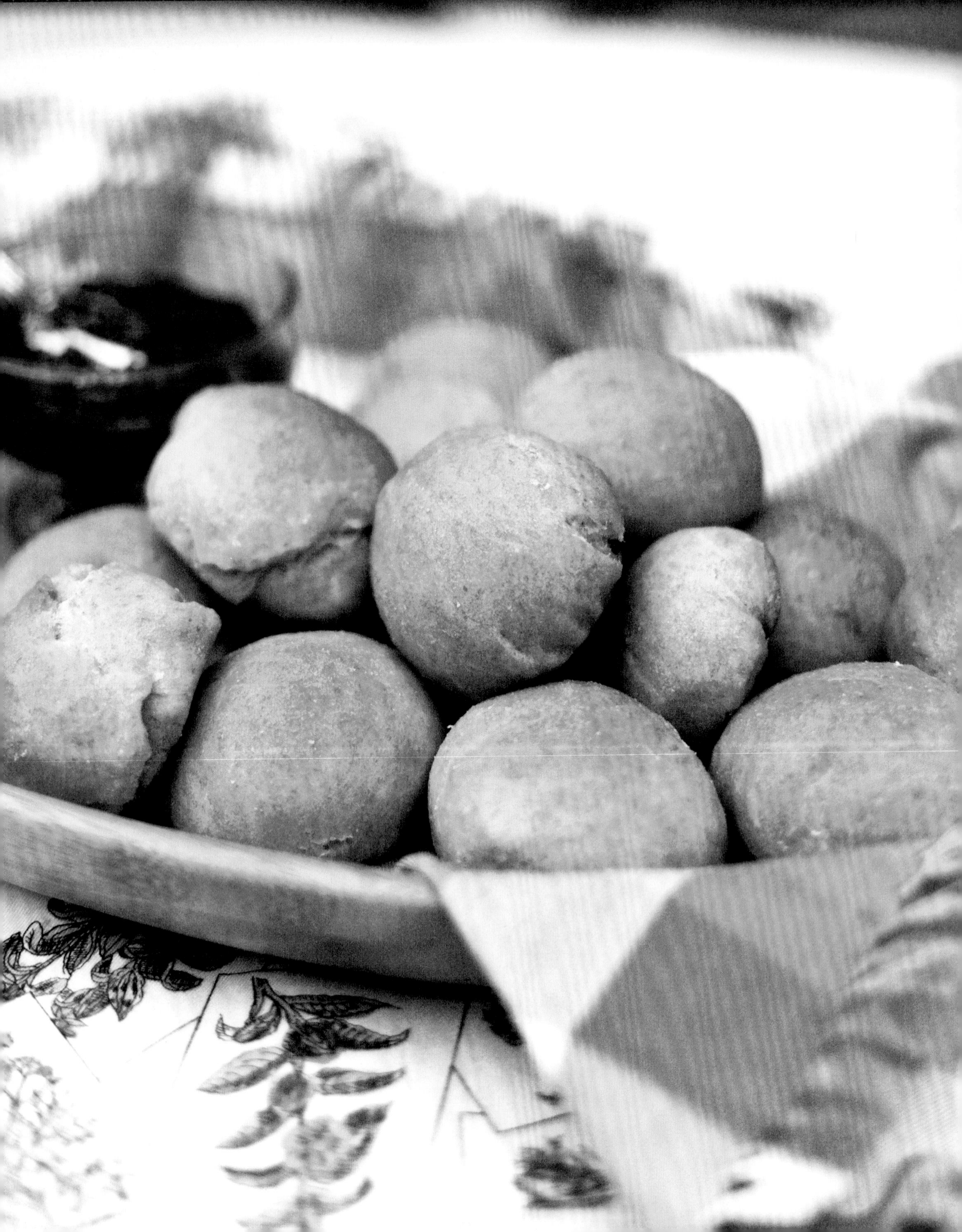

Dinner Rolls

(Using a Bread Machine)

2 C white wheat flour

1 C unbleached flour or bread flour

1 C white rye flour

3 Tbs vital wheat gluten

2 ¼ tsp salt

2 ¼ tsp yeast

1 ½ C warm water

3 Tbs honey

3 Tbs olive oil

Mix flours, vital wheat gluten, and salt in bowl. Put the water, honey, and oil into the bread pan. Then add the flour mixture, making a little well in the center, and put the yeast in the well. Close lid and put machine on the dough cycle. When cycle is finished, divide the dough into 12 evenly sized pieces and shape into rolls and place on a cookie sheet sprayed with Pam. Bake at 350° for about 20 minutes or until golden brown.

Yields: one dozen dinner rolls.

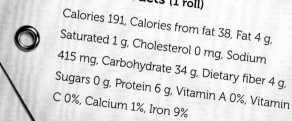

Nutrition Facts (1 roll)

Calories 191, Calories from fat 38, Fat 4 g, Saturated 1 g, Cholesterol 0 mg, Sodium 415 mg, Carbohydrate 34 g, Dietary fiber 4 g, Sugars 0 g, Protein 6 g, Vitamin A 0%, Vitamin C 0%, Calcium 1%, Iron 9%

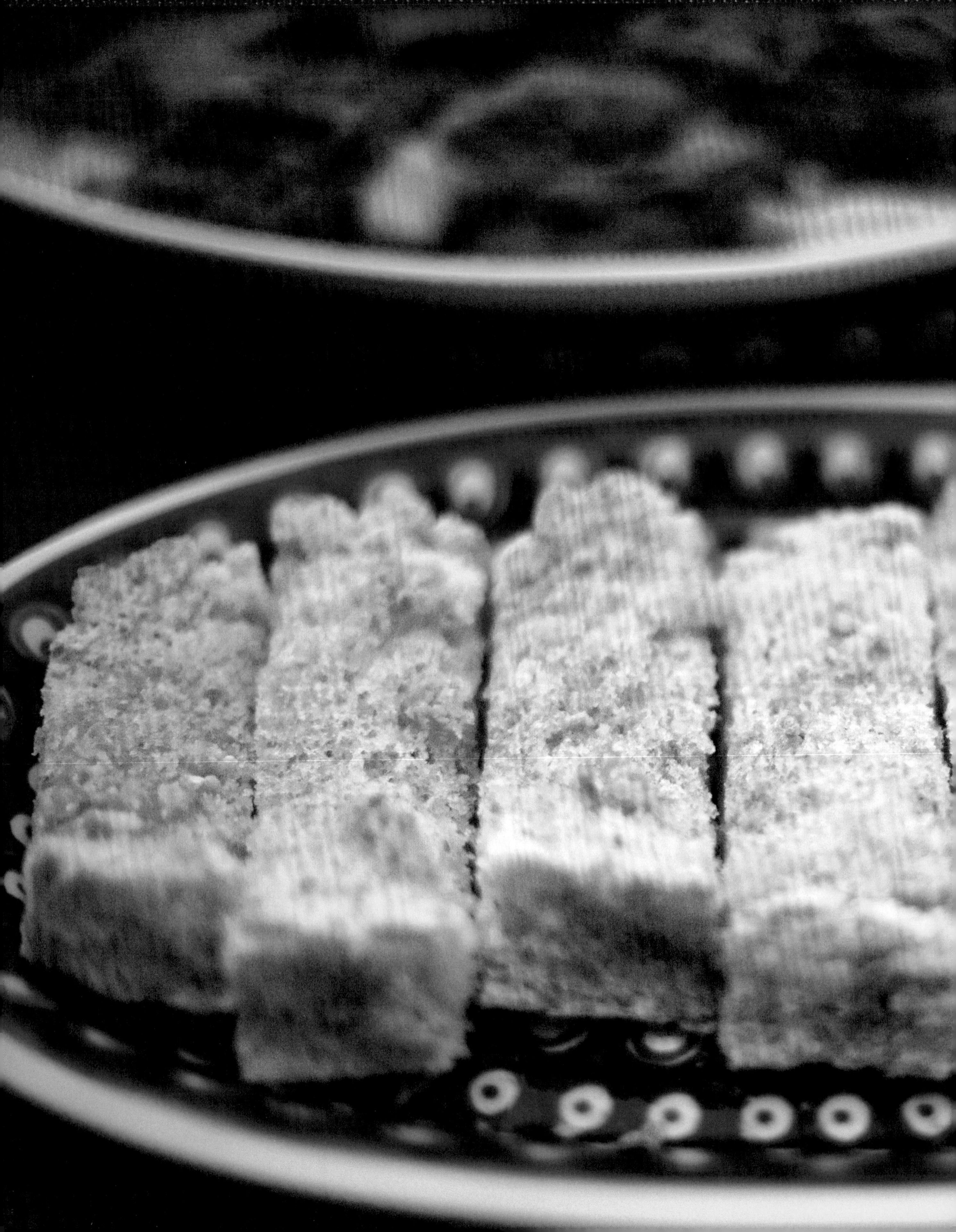

Garlic Bread

1 loaf whole wheat French bread

¼ to ½ C olive oil

3 Tbs fresh garlic, minced

3 Tbs fresh parsley, chopped

Pinch of salt

Paprika

Slice French bread horizontally. Sauté olive oil and garlic for 2 minutes. Then add salt and parsley. Spread oil with a brush on each side of the loaf. Sprinkle with paprika. Cover loaf in aluminum foil and bake at 375° for 15 minutes.

Nutrition Facts (1 slice = 1/12 loaf)

Calories 129, Fat 5 g, Saturated 1 g, Trans fat 0 g, Cholesterol 0 mg, Sodium 226 mg, Carbohydrate 18 g, Dietary fiber 1 g, Protein 1 g, Vitamin A 1%, Vitamin C 3 %, Calcium 1%, Iron 7%

Apple-Walnut Muffins

1 ½ C unbleached flour

½ C whole wheat pastry flour

1 ½ tsp Rumford baking powder

¼ tsp salt

½ tsp cinnamon

¼ tsp nutmeg

1 C organic soymilk

½ tsp vanilla

1 C maple syrup

¼ C extra light olive oil

1 small unpeeled apple

½ C walnuts, chopped

Preheat oven to 375°. Mix the dry ingredients well. Then mix the soymilk, maple syrup, olive oil, and vanilla. Add the liquid ingredients to the flour mixture and stir well. Fold in the chopped apples and chopped walnuts. Fill the cups of a 12 C muffin tin about 2/3 full. Bake for 20 - 25 minutes. Leave in the muffin tin for 5 minutes and then remove the muffins and put them on a cooling rack. (Optional topping for the muffins: 2 - 3 Tbs unbleached flour, 2 Tbs sucanat, ½ tsp cinnamon, 1 Tbs extra light olive oil. Mix with a fork until crumbly and put on top the muffins before baking them.

Nutrition Facts (1 serving = 1 muffin)

Calories 233, Fat 8 g, Saturated 1 g, Polyunsaturated 3 g, Monounsaturated 4 g, Trans fat 0 g, Cholesterol 0 mg, Sodium 173 mg, Carbohydrate 37 g, Dietary fiber 2 g, Protein 4 g, Vitamin A 2%, Vitamin C 2%, Calcium 12%, Iron 10%

Banana Bread

¾ C white wheat flour

¾ C unbleached flour

1 ½ tsp baking powder

2 heaping Tbs flax seed, ground

½ tsp salt

½ C walnuts, chopped

2 ripe bananas, mashed

1 C pure maple syrup

1 Tbs extra light olive oil

Mix the flour, baking powder, ground flax seed, and salt in one bowl. Mash the bananas and add the maple syrup, walnuts, and olive oil. Pour the banana mixture into the flour mixture and blend well. Pour batter into an oiled loaf pan and bake in a preheated 325° oven for 1 hour and 20 minutes. Leave loaf in the pan for 10 - 15 minutes, when taken out of the oven, and then cool on a wire rack. Makes 16 slices.

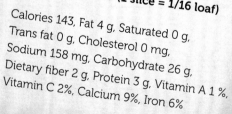

Nutrition Facts (1 slice = 1/16 loaf)

Calories 143, Fat 4 g, Saturated 0 g, Trans fat 0 g, Cholesterol 0 mg, Sodium 158 mg, Carbohydrate 26 g, Dietary fiber 2 g, Protein 3 g, Vitamin A 1 %, Vitamin C 2%, Calcium 9%, Iron 6%

Cornbread Muffins

1 C unbleached flour

1 C organic cornmeal

2 Tbs Rumford baking powder

2 Tbs organic sugar

½ tsp salt

Ener-G egg replacer for 1 egg

1 can organic creamed corn or 1 ½ C organic frozen corn pulsed in a food processor

2 Tbs melted Earth Balance margarine

½ C organic soymilk with ½ Tbs lemon juice added to make buttermilk

Mix the flour, cornmeal, baking powder, organic sugar, and salt. Follow the directions to make the equivalent of one egg with the egg replacer. Take the ½ C soymilk and add the lemon juice and let it sit for about 5 minutes, then stir. This will make buttermilk.

In another bowl put the creamed corn, egg replacer, soymilk, and melted margarine and mix well. Now add the liquid ingredients to the flour mixture and stir well. Oil a muffin pan and fill with the batter. Bake for 25 minutes at 375° or until lightly browned. Serve with Earth Balance margarine and honey. Very yummy!

Makes 12 muffins.

Nutrition Facts (1 muffin)

Calories 130, Fat 3 g, Saturated 1 g, Polyunsaturated 1 g, Monounsaturated 1 g, Trans fat 0 g, Cholesterol 0 mg, Sodium 668 mg, Carbohydrate 25 g, Dietary fiber 2 g, Protein 3 g, Vitamin A 1%, Vitamin C 3%, Calcium 34%, Iron 7%

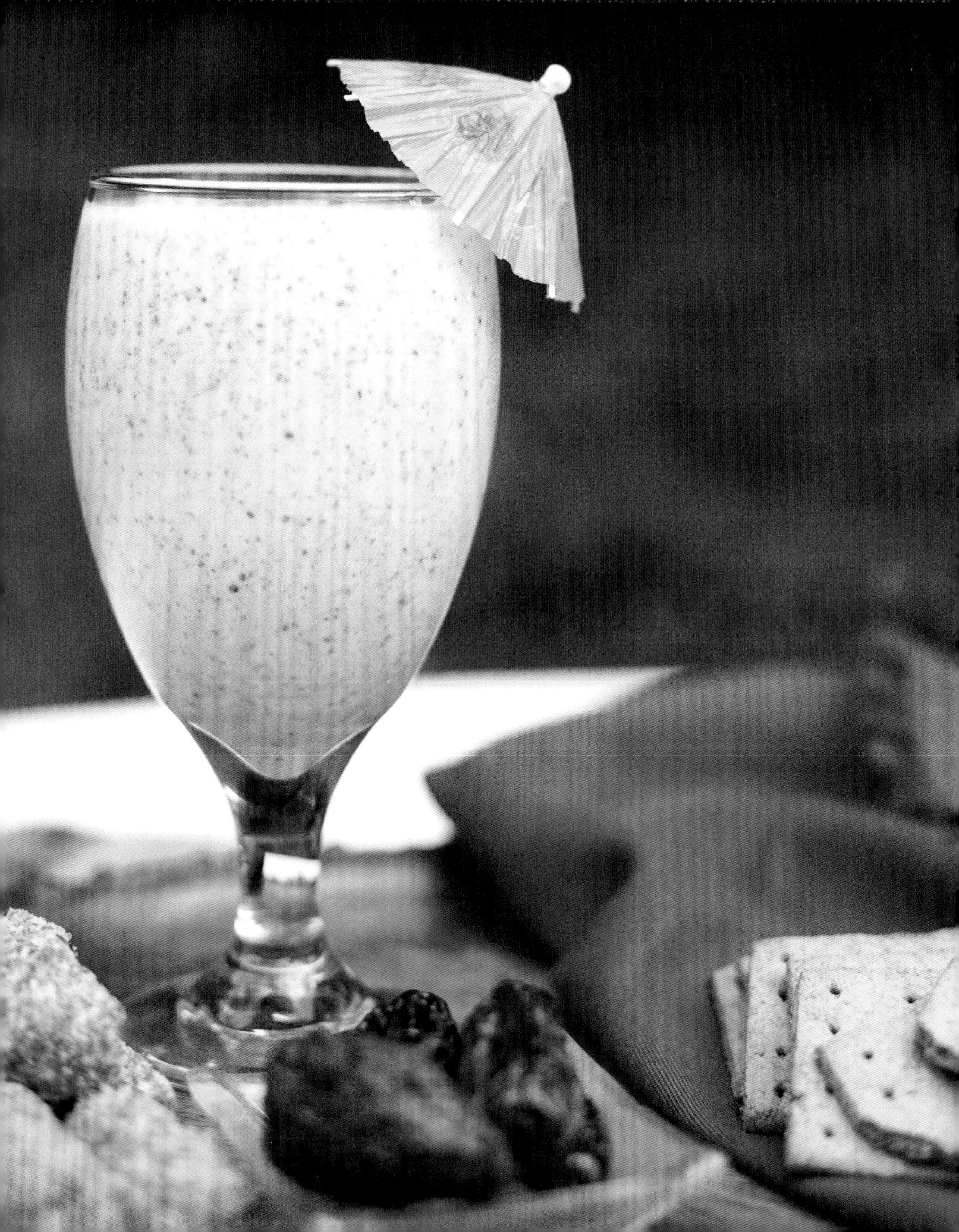

Date Shakes

2/3 C pitted dates

1 ½ C organic vanilla soymilk

1 - 1 ½ frozen banana chunks

Blend all in the blender. Serves 3. Hint: If you don't have a Vitamix or Blendtec blender, you will need to cook the dates in a little water before blending so they will blend easily. In California dates are plentiful, and usually this shake is made with real ice cream—the frozen bananas work great, and it tastes just as good! (No oxidized cholesterol in these shakes!)

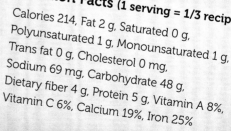

Nutrition Facts (1 serving = 1/3 recipe)

Calories 214, Fat 2 g, Saturated 0 g,
Polyunsaturated 1 g, Monounsaturated 1 g,
Trans fat 0 g, Cholesterol 0 mg,
Sodium 69 mg, Carbohydrate 48 g,
Dietary fiber 4 g, Protein 5 g, Vitamin A 8%,
Vitamin C 6%, Calcium 19%, Iron 25%

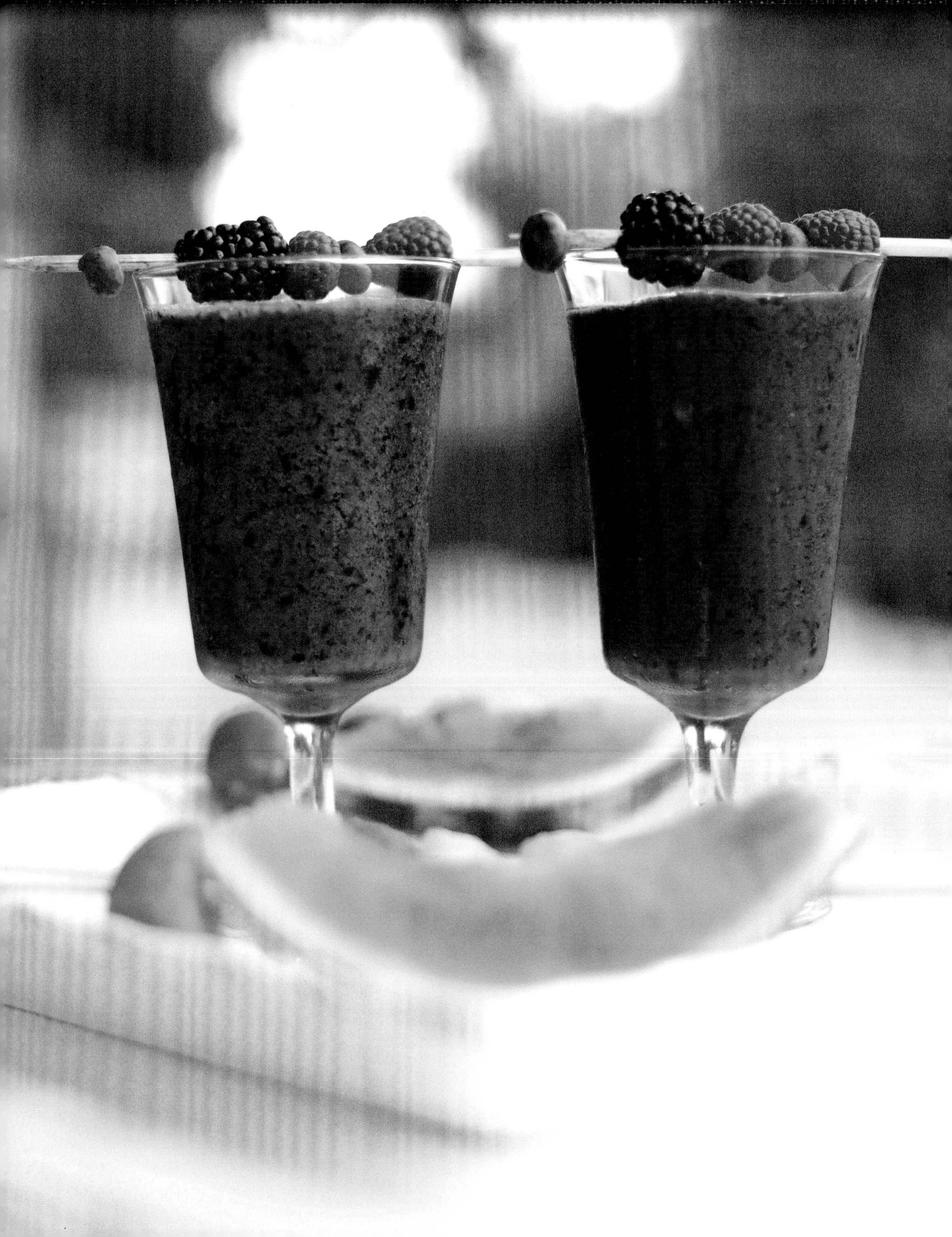

Fruit Smoothies

1 banana, frozen in chunks

½ C frozen strawberries

½ C frozen blueberries

½ C frozen raspberries

1 - 1 ½ C organic soymilk

1 Tbs pure maple syrup (optional)

Blend all ingredients in blender. Serves 3.

Nutrition Facts (1 serving = 1/3 recipe)
Calories 120, Fat 2 g, Saturated 0 g,
Trans fat 0 g, Cholesterol 0 mg,
Sodium 57 mg, Carbohydrate 22 g,
Dietary fiber 5 g, Protein 6 g, Vitamin A 5%,
Vitamin C 29%, Calcium 6%, Iron 10%

Piña Coladas

1 ½ C pineapple juice

1 C frozen pineapple chunks

½ C coconut milk

1 Tbs flaked coconut

Blend all ingredients in the blender and top with toasted coconut shavings. Serves 2.

Optional: You can add ¼ - ½ C of vanilla soy ice cream, if desired

Nutrition Facts (1 serving = ½ recipe)

Calories 254, Fat 5 g, Saturated 4 g,
Trans fat 0 g, Cholesterol 0 mg,
Sodium 11 mg, Carbohydrate 51 g,
Dietary fiber 2 g, Protein 1 g, Vitamin A 1%,
Vitamin C 123%, Calcium 4%, Iron 8%

Cappuccino

2 cups organic vanilla soymilk

2 tablespoons maple syrup

2 teaspoons powdered coffee substitute (Roma or Pero)

½ teaspoon vanilla extract

Briefly blend all ingredients in the blender. Serve hot or chilled.
Makes 2 servings.

Hint: You can top with whipped topping and a sprinkle of cinnamon.
This recipe is from the cookbook *The Total Vegetarian*, by Barbara Watson.

Nutrition Facts (per 8-oz serving)

Calories 179 , Protein 9.2 g,

Carbohydrates 25.7 g, Dietary fiber 3.2 g,

Fat 5.1 g, Sodium 32 mg

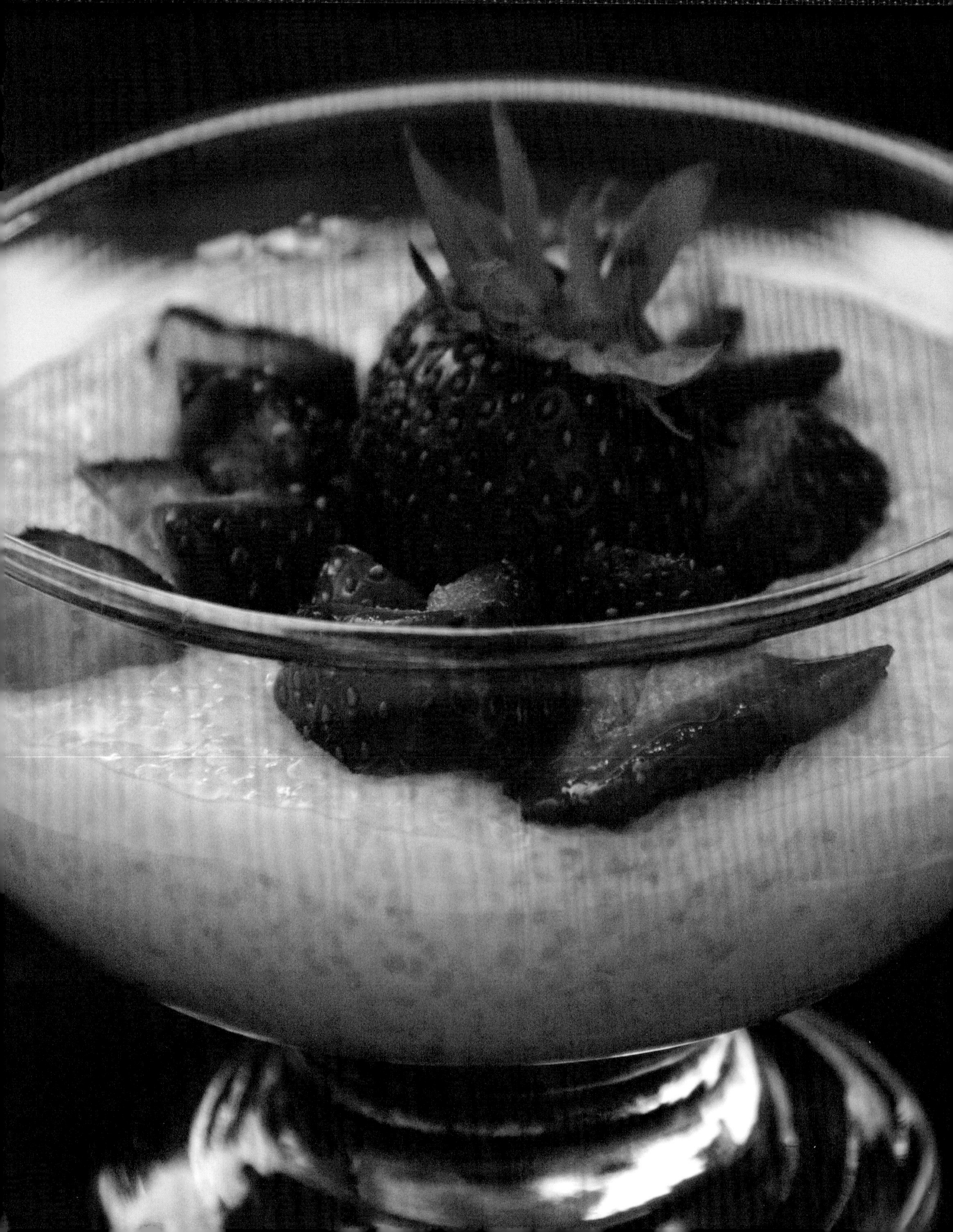

Tapioca Pudding

1 can light coconut milk

1/3 C quick tapioca

¾ C organic soymilk

¼ C maple syrup

Pinch of salt

½ vanilla bean seed (or ½ tsp extract)

Top with toasted coconut or fresh berries

Cook all ingredients, through the salt, at medium heat until it reaches a full boil. When pudding is cool, add the seeds from the vanilla bean. Top with coconut or fresh berries. Berries add more fiber to this dessert: ½ C of berries can add 1 ½ gm to 4 gm of fiber.

Serves 4.

Nutrition Facts (1 serving = ¼ recipe)

Calories 201, Fat 9 g, Saturated 7 g,
Trans fat 0 g, Cholesterol 0 mg,
Sodium 72 mg, Carbohydrate 26 g,
Dietary fiber 1 g, Protein 2 g, Vitamin A 3%,
Vitamin C 0%, Calcium 4%, Iron 8%

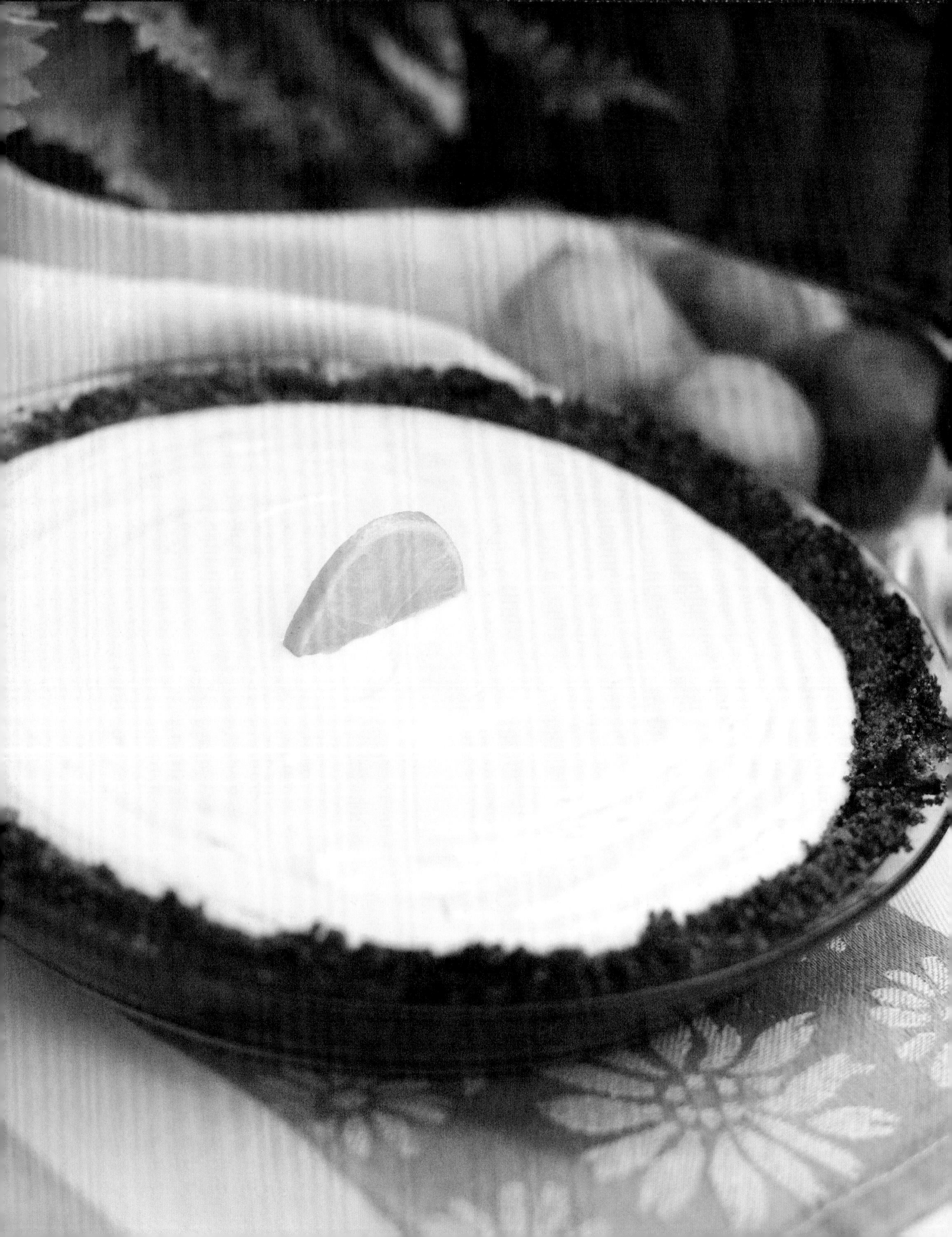

Key Lime Pie

Pie Filling

1 pkg Follow Your Heart cream cheese (8 oz.)

½ C lime juice (can use lemon if you don't have limes)

2 pkg Mori-nu lemon or vanilla crème pudding mix

1 Tbs honey

1 pkg organic Mori-nu light extra-firm tofu

2 Tbs organic sugar

Blend in blender and pour into graham cracker crust.

Graham Cracker Crust

1 ½ C graham crackers, crushed

2 Tbs extra light olive oil

4 Tbs pure maple syrup

Mix ingredients together until well combined. Then press mixture into the bottom and up the sides of a 9-in pie plate or tin.

Hint: Arrowhead Mills makes a graham cracker crust that's free of trans fats.

Nutrition Facts (1 slice = 1/8 pie)
Calories 351, Fat 18 g, Saturated 5 g,
Trans fat 0 g, Cholesterol 0 mg,
Sodium 280 mg, Carbohydrate 42 g,
Dietary fiber 1 g, Protein 5 g, Vitamin A 1%,
Vitamin C 2%, Calcium 3%, Iron 6%

Apple Pie

6 - 7 apples, peeled and sliced

1/3 C frozen apple juice concentrate

2 Tbs unbleached flour

1 tsp cinnamon

¼ tsp nutmeg

2 Tbs organic sugar (optional)

Double crust unbaked pie crust

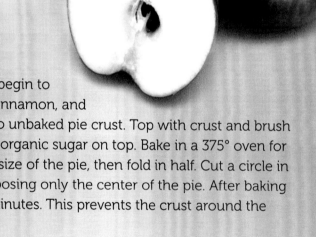

Mix apples with apple juice concentrate. If apples begin to brown, just add a twist of lemon juice. Mix flour, cinnamon, and nutmeg and add to apple mixture. Pour apples into unbaked pie crust. Top with crust and brush the top crust with a little water and sprinkle some organic sugar on top. Bake in a 375° oven for one hour. I use aluminum foil and cut a piece the size of the pie, then fold in half. Cut a circle in the center of the foil and put it around the pie, exposing only the center of the pie. After baking for 40 minutes, remove foil and bake the last 20 minutes. This prevents the crust around the edge from getting too dark.

Hint: Many store-bought frozen pie crusts are made with lard. Make your own or check the ingredients.

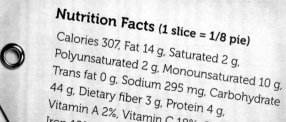

Nutrition Facts (1 slice = 1/8 pie)
Calories 307, Fat 14 g, Saturated 2 g, Polyunsaturated 2 g, Monounsaturated 10 g, Trans fat 0 g, Sodium 295 mg, Carbohydrate 44 g, Dietary fiber 3 g, Protein 4 g, Vitamin A 2%, Vitamin C 18%, Calcium 3%, Iron 10%

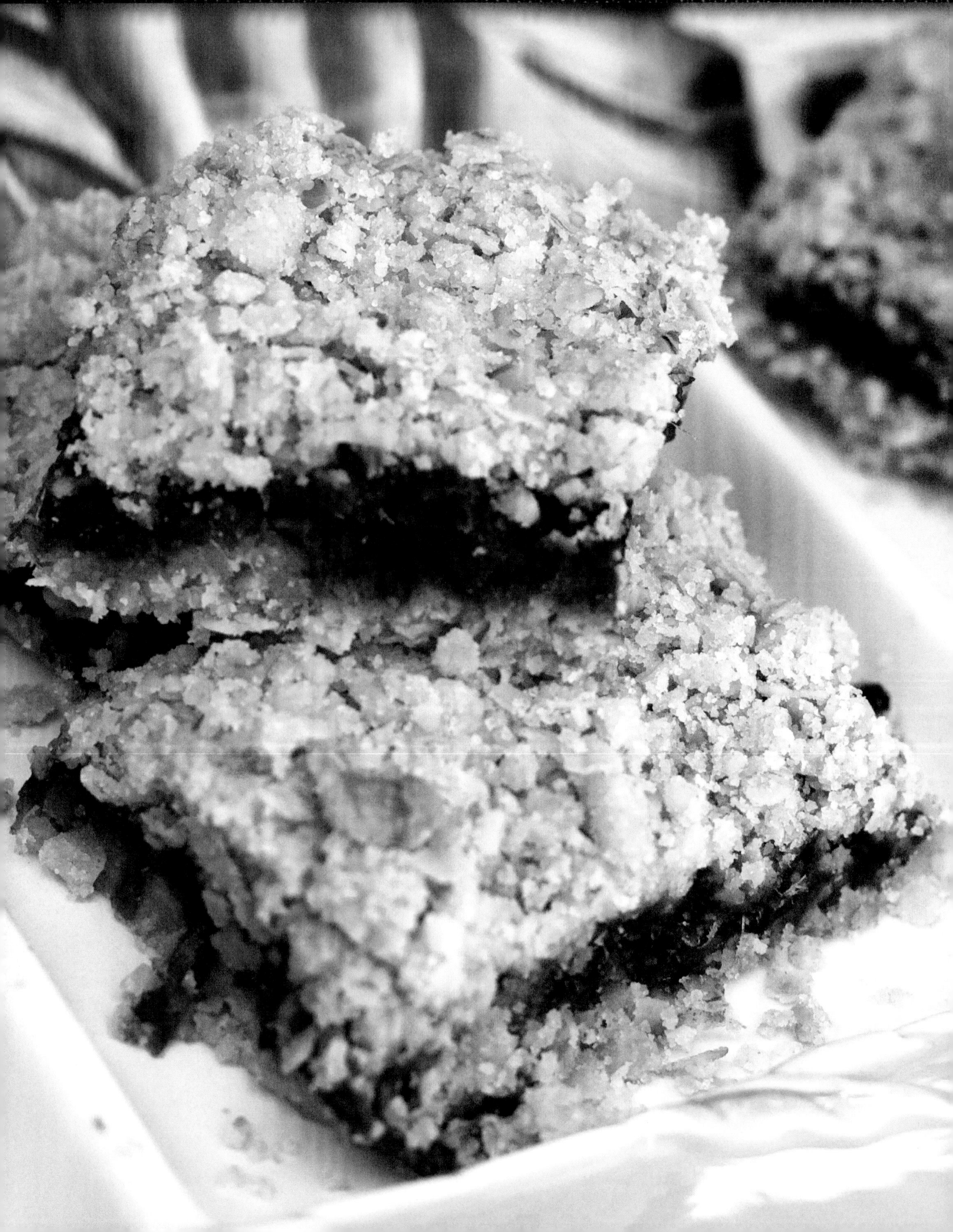

Date Bars

Outer Layers

1 ½ C whole wheat pastry flour

1 ½ C quick oats

½ tsp salt

½ C chopped walnuts

1 - 2 Tbs water

½ C extra light olive oil

½ C organic sugar

Date Filling

2 ½ C pitted dates

2 ½ C water

Combine flour, oats, salt, water, and walnuts. In a separate bowl mix the olive oil and sucanat. Add the olive oil mixture to the flour. Press half of the mixture into the baking dish. Cook the dates in the water until they can be mashed into a paste. Let the dates cool. Spread the date paste over the crumb mixture. Then spread the rest of the crumb mixture over the dates and press it gently. Bake at 350° for 25 minutes. Makes about 25 bars.

Nutrition Facts (1 serving = 1 bar)

Calories 159, Fat 6 g, Saturated 1 g, Polyunsaturated 1 g Monounsaturated 4 g Trans fat 0 g, Cholesterol 0 mg, Sodium 48 mg, Carbohydrate 26 g, Dietary fiber 3 g, Sugars 15 g, Protein 3 g, Vitamin A 1%, Vitamin C 1%, Calcium 2%, Iron 5%

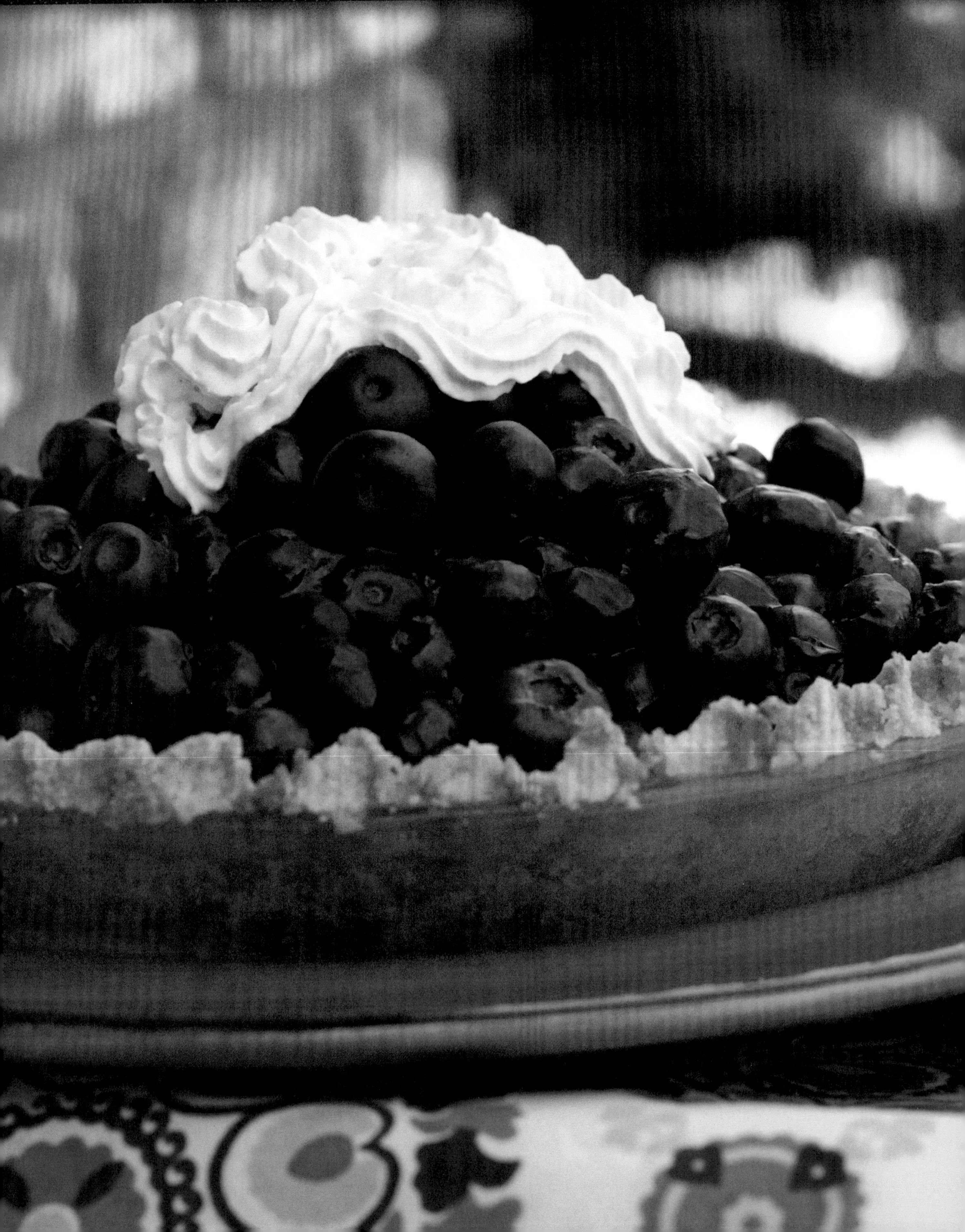

Fresh Blueberry Pie

Pie Filling

4 ½ C blueberries

½ C water

2 Tbs organic cornstarch

½ – ¾ C brown sugar

½ tsp lemon juice

Mix ½ C blueberries, ½ C water,
cornstarch, and brown sugar in saucepan. Bring
to a boil and cook until thickened. Cool slightly. Add remaining
berries and lemon juice. Pour into baked pie shell. Chill and serve.

Pie Crust

1 C unbleached flour

½ C whole wheat pastry flour

2 Tbs organic sugar

2 Tbs organic soymilk

1 tsp salt

½ C extra light olive oil

Mix and pat into pie pan. Bake 20 - 30 minutes
at 350°. After the crust cools, add blueberry filling.

*Hint: Top with Soyatoo Soy Whip or Rice Whip topping, available at
most health food stores.*

Nutrition Facts (1 slice = 1/8 pie)
Calories 320, Fat 14 g, Saturated 2 g,
Polyunsaturated 2 g, Monounsaturated 10 g,
Trans fat 0 g, Cholesterol 0 mg,
Sodium 300 mg, Carbohydrate 48 g,
Dietary fiber 3 g, Protein 3 g, Vitamin A 1%,
Vitamin 11%, Calcium 3%, Iron 10%

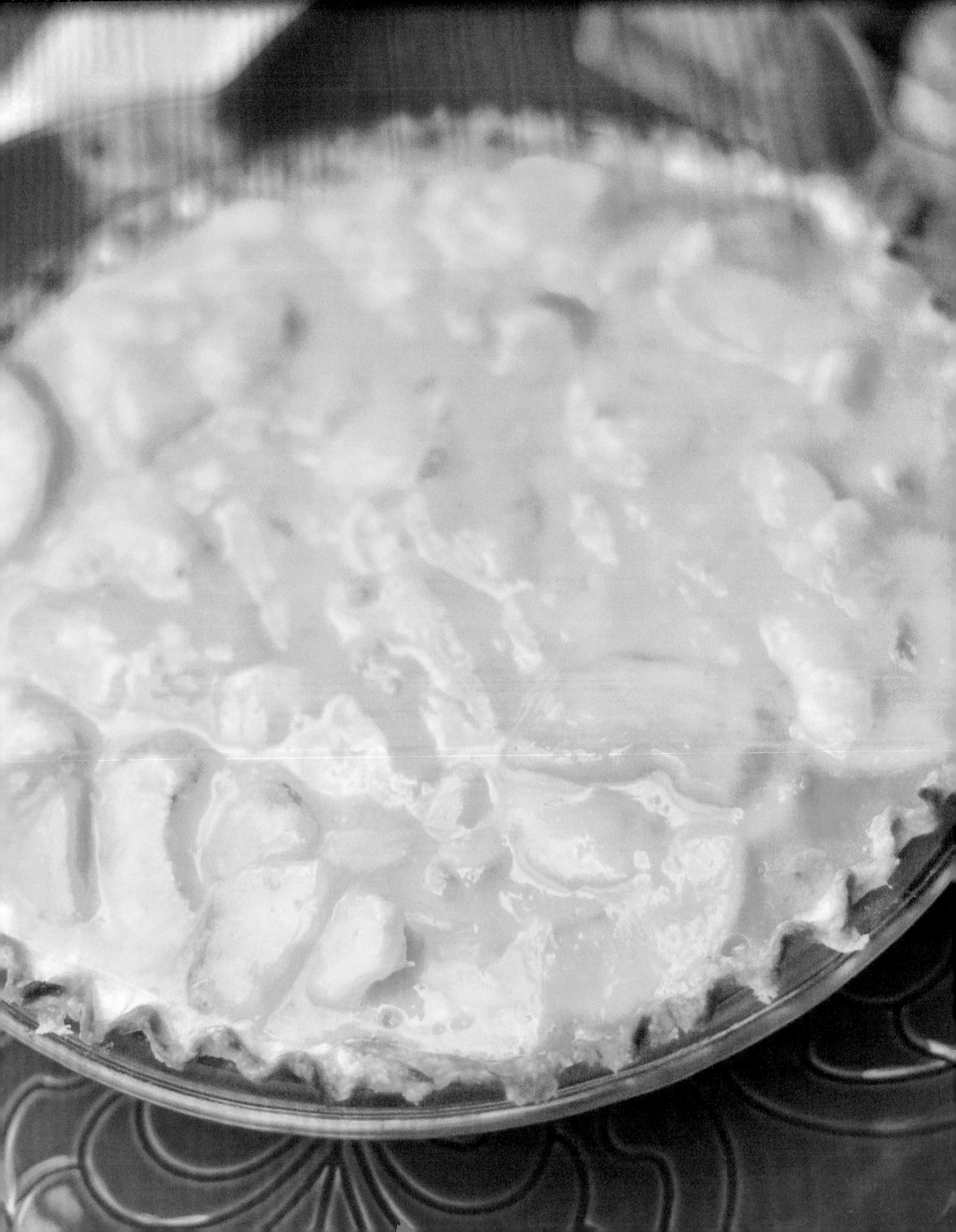

Fresh Peach Pie

1 9-in single pie crust, baked

4 oz Follow Your Heart cream cheese, softened

¾ C organic sugar

6 ½ C firm-ripe peaches, sliced, peeled

¾ C orange juice

1/3 C organic cornstarch

1 Tbs lemon juice

Mix Better Than Cream Cheese with
¼ C organic sugar until smooth. Spread evenly
over cooled, baked pie crust. In blender whirl
1 C sliced peaches, remaining ½ C fructose, orange
juice, and cornstarch until smooth. Pour into kettle and
cook over medium-high heat until it boils and thickens.
Remove from heat and stir in lemon juice.

Add remaining peaches to hot peach glaze and gently mix to
coat slices. Let cool. Pour peach mixture onto cream cheese in pie crust. Refrigerate.

*Serving Tip: Chill uncovered until firm enough to cut—at least 3 hours.
Serve with whipped topping flavored with orange zest.*

Nutrition Facts (1 slice = 1/8 pie)
Calories 300, Fat 11 g, Saturated Fat 2 g,
Polyunsaturated 4 g, Monounsaturated 5 g,
Trans fat 0 g, Cholesterol 0 mg,
Sodium 214 mg, Carbohydrate 49 g,
Dietary fiber 3 g, Protein 4 g, Vitamin A 4%,
Vitamin C 25%, Calcium 2%, Iron 6%

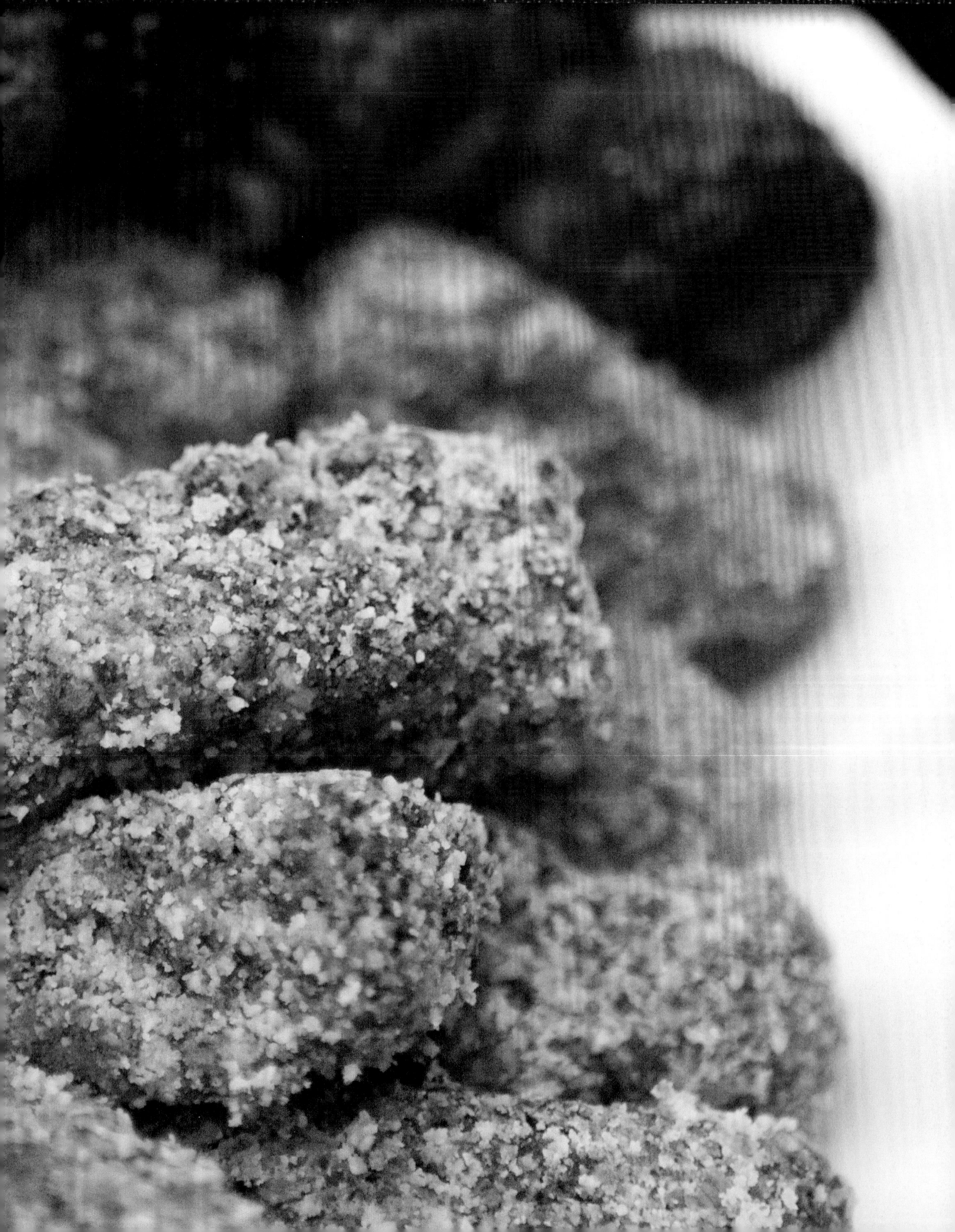

Fruit & Nut Bars

1 C walnuts

1 C organic raisins

2 Tbs raw sunflower seeds

1 Tbs water

Almond meal

In a food processor, grind the sunflower seeds and walnuts. When the nuts and seeds are finely ground, add the raisins and grind. When the fruit and nuts are both finely ground, put them in a bowl and add 1 Tbs of water.

Mix thoroughly. Shape the mixture into bars and roll in almond meal. A tasty, raw dessert. Makes 12 bars.

Nutrition Facts (1 serving = 1 bar)

Calories 136, Fat 9 g, Saturated 1 g, Trans fat 0 g, Cholesterol 0 mg, Sodium 2 mg, Carbohydrate 12 g, Dietary fiber 2 g, Sugars 7 g, Protein 4 g, Vitamin A 1%, Vitamin C 1%, Calcium 3%, Iron 5%

Mangos & Sticky Rice

2 C jasmine brown rice

½ C organic sugar

1 can coconut milk

2 mangos, peeled, pitted

Put rice in a strainer and wash until the water is clear. Then put the rice in a bowl and cover with cold water and let it soak overnight or 8 hours or more. Then cook the rice until tender.

Heat the coconut milk in a kettle and add the organic sugar. Bring to a boil and stir. Reduce heat, cover, and simmer for about 5 minutes until slightly thickened.

Pour coconut milk over the rice and fluff with a fork. Cover and let it sit for 15 minutes. Scoop a mound of rice onto each plate and serve with fresh sliced mangos. Serves 4.

Hint: Before serving, you can add some cream of coconut—about 1/3 C—to the rice. It makes it more sticky and sweet. Very yummy! Cream of coconut can be found in Asian markets.

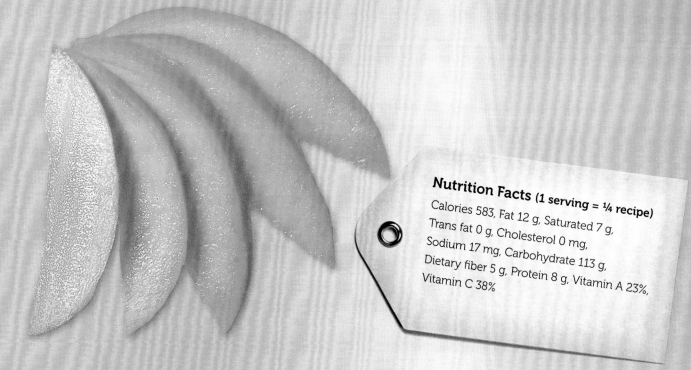

Nutrition Facts (1 serving = ¼ recipe)
Calories 583, Fat 12 g, Saturated 7 g,
Trans fat 0 g, Cholesterol 0 mg,
Sodium 17 mg, Carbohydrate 113 g,
Dietary fiber 5 g, Protein 8 g, Vitamin A 23%,
Vitamin C 38%

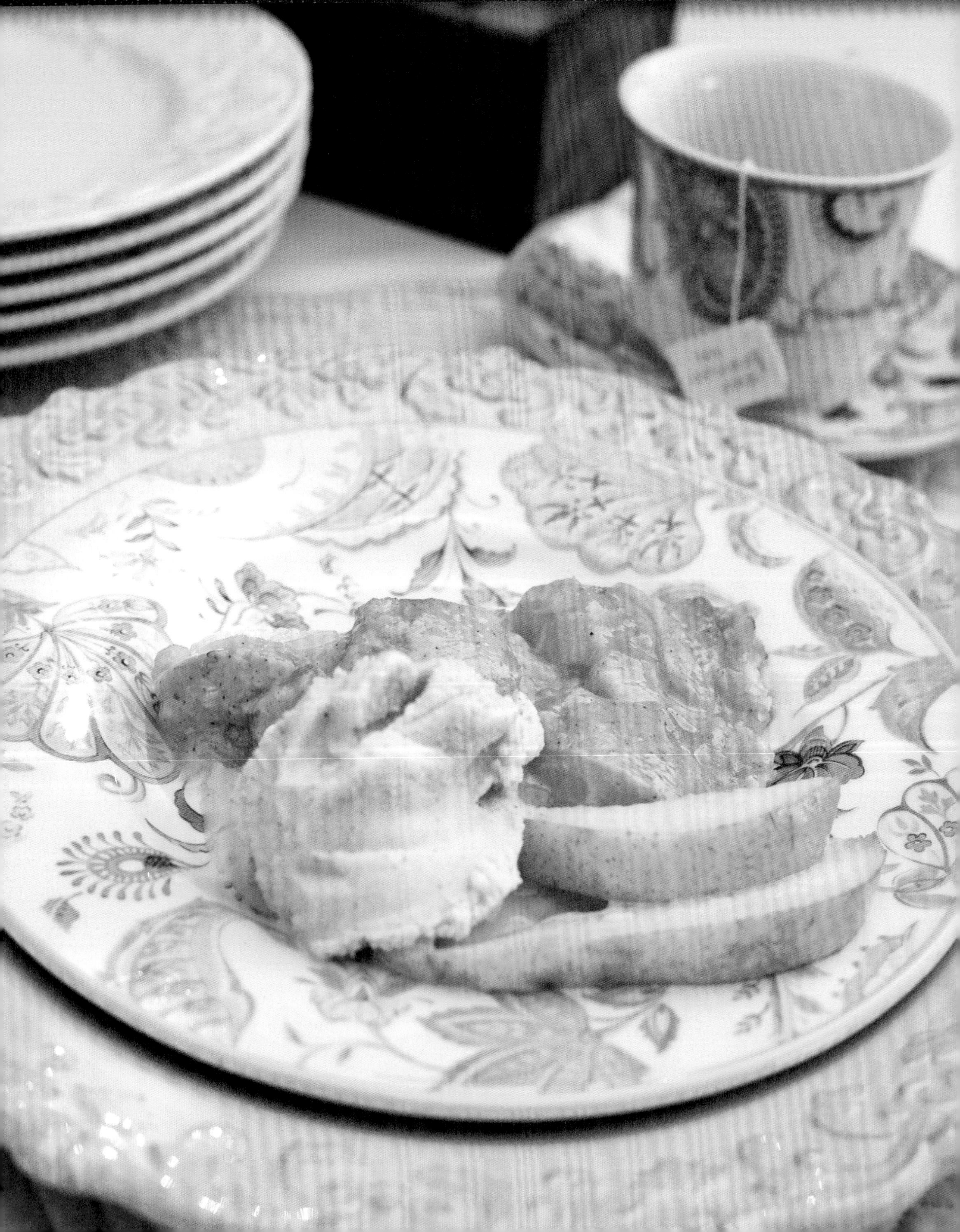

Pear Pie

5 - 6 pears, peeled

¾ C organic sugar

4 Tbs unbleached flour

½ tsp nutmeg

¼ tsp cinnamon

1 C organic soy creamer

1 unbaked pie crust

Peel and slice the pears so they lie flat in the unbaked pie shell. Mix the flour with the spices and add the creamer. Pour the flour mixture over the pears and bake at 350° for about 50 minutes.

Serve warm with organic vanilla soy ice cream.

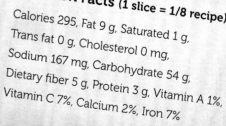

Nutrition Facts (1 slice = 1/8 recipe)
Calories 295, Fat 9 g, Saturated 1 g,
Trans fat 0 g, Cholesterol 0 mg,
Sodium 167 mg, Carbohydrate 54 g,
Dietary fiber 5 g, Protein 3 g, Vitamin A 1%,
Vitamin C 7%, Calcium 2%, Iron 7%

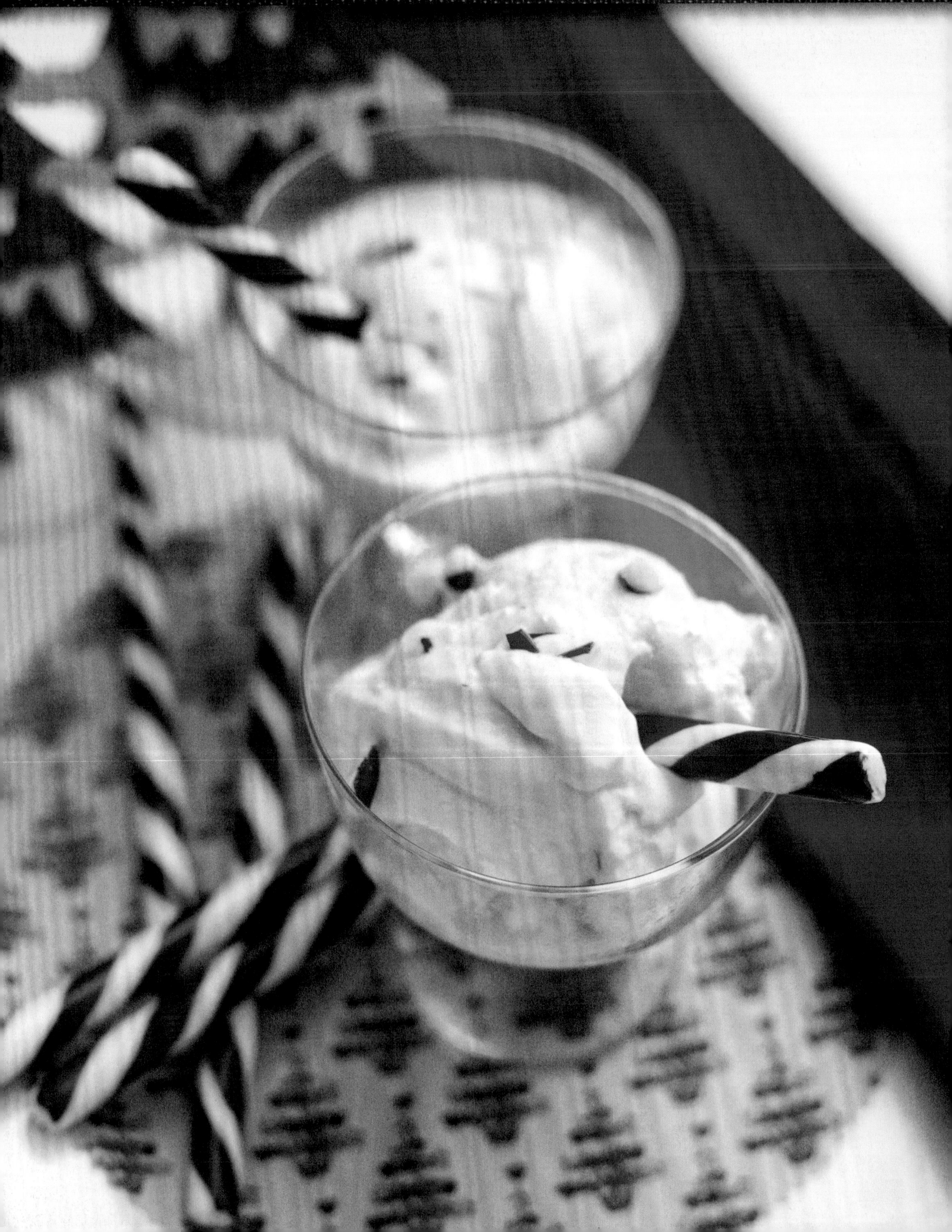

Peppermint Ice Cream

2 pts organic soy creamer

½ - 1 tsp peppermint extract

½ C organic sugar

Pinch of salt

½ peppermint stick, crushed

Mix the soy creamer, extract, organic sugar, and salt in a pitcher and refrigerate. When you're ready to make the ice cream, pour it into the frozen tub and turn the machine on. After the ice cream is beginning to thicken, add the crushed peppermint candy (you will only need ½ - 1 whole peppermint stick for one batch of ice cream).

This is a fun ice cream to make for the holidays.

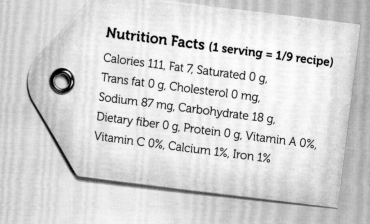

Nutrition Facts (1 serving = 1/9 recipe)

Calories 111, Fat 7, Saturated 0 g, Trans fat 0 g, Cholesterol 0 mg, Sodium 87 mg, Carbohydrate 18 g, Dietary fiber 0 g, Protein 0 g, Vitamin A 0%, Vitamin C 0%, Calcium 1%, Iron 1%

Pumpkin Dip

½ C canned pumpkin

1/3 C brown sugar

½ C Follow Your Heart cream cheese, softened

1 Tbs maple syrup

1 tsp cinnamon

½ tsp pumpkin pie spice or nutmeg

Combine cream cheese, pumpkin, and brown sugar with an electric mixer on medium speed until blended well. Add cinnamon, pumpkin pie spice or nutmeg, and maple syrup and beat until smooth. Cover and chill for 30 minutes. Use as a dip for apple or pear slices.

Nutrition Facts (1 serving = 2 Tbs)

Calories 90, Fat 3 g, Saturated 1 g, Trans fat 0 g, Cholesterol 0 mg, Sodium 121 mg, Potassium 70 mg, Carbohydrates 17 g Dietary fiber 1 g, Sugars 12 g, Protein 7 g, Vitamin A 17%, Vitamin C 1%, Calcium 2%, Iron 3%

Pumpkin Pie

1 14-oz can pureed pumpkin

1 C organic vanilla soymilk

½ C pure maple syrup

½ C organic sugar

3 Tbs organic cornstarch

½ tsp salt

½ tsp cinnamon

1 tsp pumpkin pie spice

1 unbaked pie crust

Mix canned pumpkin, soymilk, maple syrup, organic sugar, cornstarch, salt, and spices. You can blend in blender or mix with an electric mixer. Pour into an unbaked pie shell and bake for 1 hour in a preheated oven of 350°. Let the pie cool on a cooling rack before refrigerating. The pie will get more firm as it cools. Top with non-dairy whipped topping. Serves 8.

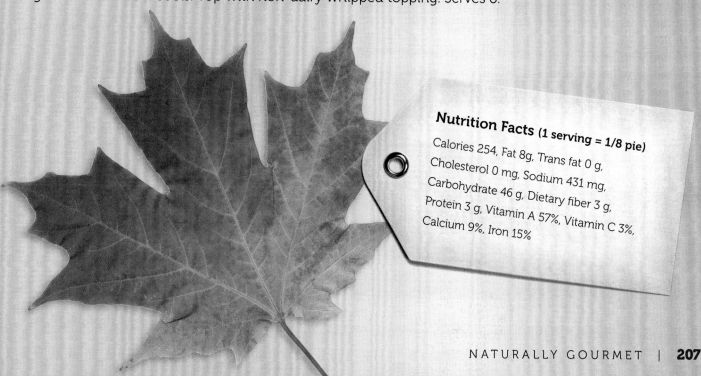

Nutrition Facts (1 serving = 1/8 pie)

Calories 254, Fat 8g, Trans fat 0 g, Cholesterol 0 mg, Sodium 431 mg, Carbohydrate 46 g, Dietary fiber 3 g, Protein 3 g, Vitamin A 57%, Vitamin C 3%, Calcium 9%, Iron 15%

Strawberry-Rhubarb Pie

1 recipe double pie crust

2 C rhubarb, chopped

4 C fresh strawberries, sliced

2/3 C organic sugar

1/3 C unbleached flour

½ tsp cinnamon

Prepare pastry dough for the crust and
put in 9-in pie plate. In a bowl stir together
flour, sucanat, and cinnamon and mix well. Add
strawberries and rhubarb and gently toss together. Pour
fruit mixture into pie crust and top with the remaining crust.

Use aluminum foil cut the size of the pie and cut a circle out in the center of
the foil. Put foil over the pie, exposing the center of the crust. Bake for 25 minutes at 375 degrees.
Then remove the foil and bake for 25 minutes longer or until the crust is nicely browned. Cool
on a wire rack.

Nutrition Facts (1 serving = 1/8 pie)

Calories 334, Fat 14 g, Saturated 2 g,
Polyunsaturated 2 g, Monounsaturated 10 g,
Trans fat 0 g, Cholesterol 0 mg, Sodium 294
mg, Carbohydrate 50 g, Dietary fiber 4 g,
Protein 5 g, Vitamin A 1%, Vitamin C 60%,
Calcium 6%, Iron 11%

Almond Delight Ice Cream Pie

Almond Crust

1 ½ C toasted almonds, chopped

1 Tbs extra light olive oil

1 ½ Tbs honey

Coat an 8 x 8-in pan with non-stick spray. Mix the crust ingredients and press the mixture firmly onto the bottom and sides of the pan. Then put the pan in the freezer and freeze while preparing the filling.

Filling

¼ C unsweetened, finely shredded coconut, lightly toasted

1 Tbs honey

½ C almond or peanut butter

3 Tbs toasted almonds, chopped

2 pints organic vanilla soy ice cream (p. 213), optional: vanilla coconut ice cream

In a small bowl mix the coconut, honey, almond butter, and almonds. Place the ice cream in a large bowl and stir to soften. Stir in the almond mixture. Spoon into the chilled crust. Sprinkle additional toasted coconut over pie. Freeze for at least 2 hours or until firm. You can cut the pieces to whatever size you wish, so you can serve anywhere from 8 - 12. This recipe is from *Depression, the Way Out*.

Nutrition Facts (1 serving = 1/10 recipe)

Calories 362, Fat 25 g, Saturated 3 g, Trans fat 0 g, Cholesterol 0 mg, Sodium 103 mg, Carbohydrate 31 g, **Dietary fiber 6 g**, Protein 8 g, Vitamin A 0%, Vitamin C 1%, Calcium 10%, Iron 11%

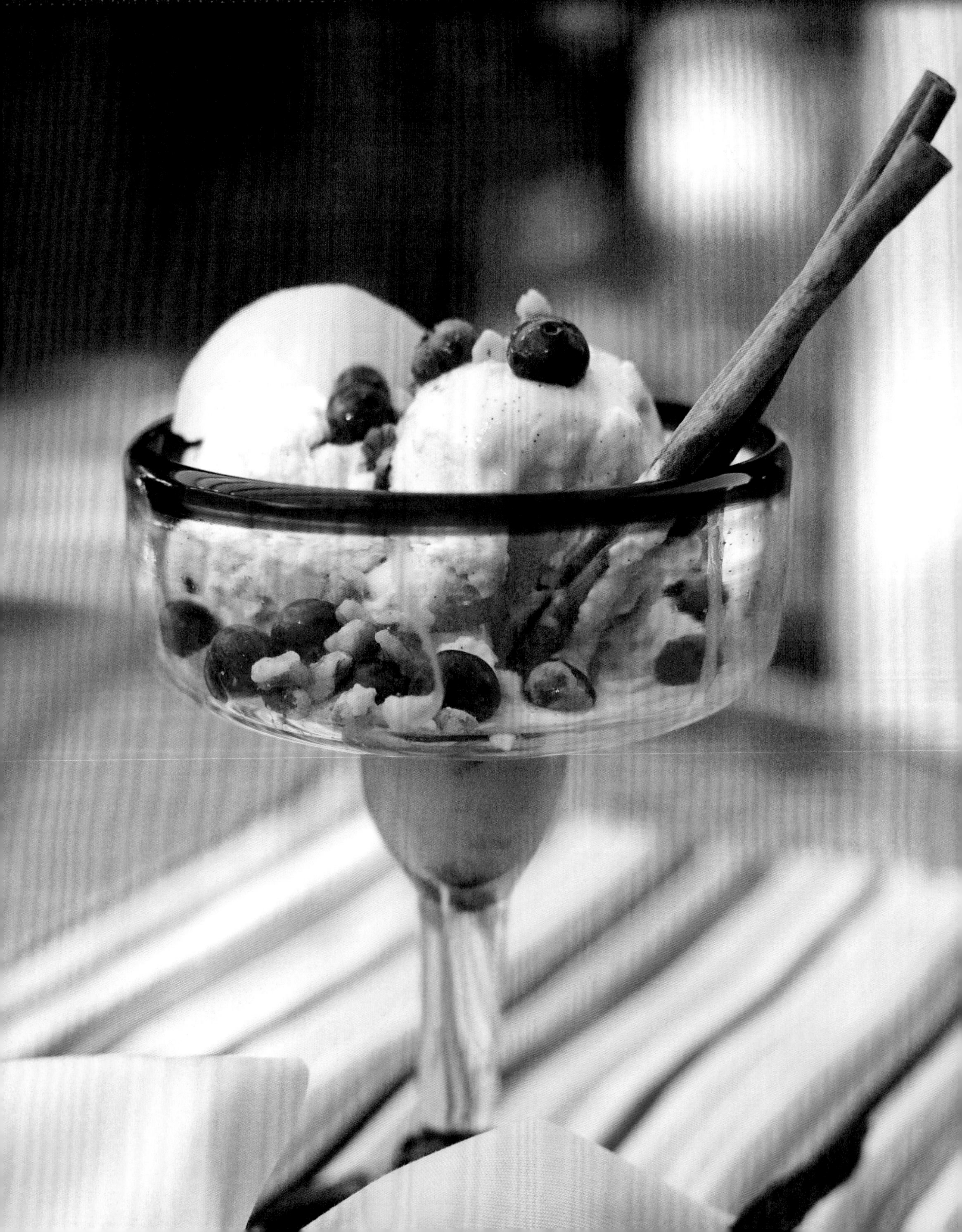

Vanilla Ice Cream

2 pts organic soy creamer

½ C organic sugar

Pinch of salt

1 - 2 vanilla beans (scrape the seeds out)—or 1 tsp vanilla bean paste or extract

Put the ice cream tub in the freezer 24 hours prior to making ice cream. Mix the creamer, organic sugar, pinch of salt, and vanilla seeds together and put in a pitcher in the refrigerator so it gets cold.

When ready to make the ice cream, shake the pitcher with the creamer and pour into the ice cream maker tub. Turn on the machine, and within 20 - 30 minutes, your ice cream will be ready. One quart serves about 9 single-scoop servings.

Top with fresh fruit and nuts—this will add fiber and flavor to the dessert.

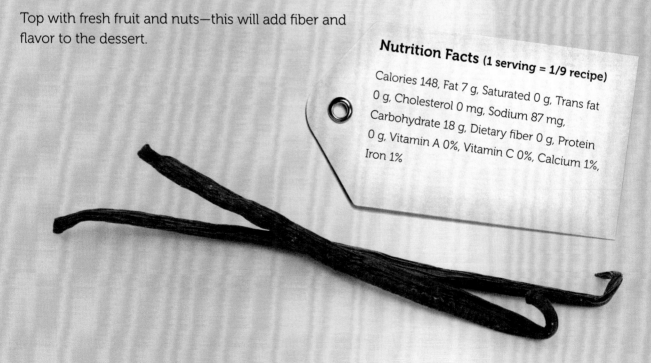

Nutrition Facts (1 serving = 1/9 recipe)

Calories 148, Fat 7 g, Saturated 0 g, Trans fat 0 g, Cholesterol 0 mg, Sodium 87 mg, Carbohydrate 18 g, Dietary fiber 0 g, Protein 0 g, Vitamin A 0%, Vitamin C 0%, Calcium 1%, Iron 1%

Pie Crust

1 C unbleached flour

1 C whole wheat pastry flour

1/2 C extra light olive oil

1 tsp salt

½ C boiling water

Mix salt and flour. Pour water and oil in, all at once. Stir with a fork. Roll between 2 sheets of waxed paper. Remove top paper. Lay crust side down. After putting the top crust on the pie, flute the edges. This is a double pie crust. Bake as pie recipe indicates.

Hint: You can vary the whole wheat pastry flour to use more or less, as long as the total flour measurement comes to 2 cups.

Nutrition Facts (1 serving = 1/8 recipe)

Calories 225, Fat 14 g, Saturated 2 g, Polyunsaturated 2 g, Monounsaturated 10 g, Trans fat 0 g, Cholesterol 0 mg, Sodium 292 mg, Carbohydrate 23 g, Dietary fiber 2 g, Protein 4 g, Vitamin A 0%, Vitamin C 0%, Calcium 2%, Iron 8%

First Class Foods

'Old Tom Parr" was an Englishman born in 1483, when the country's average lifespan was 32. But Tom was far from average. He lived to the ripe old age of 152. Curious about Tom's health secret, King Charles invited him to a two-week vacation at the royal palace. During the visit, Tom feasted on rich delicacies. The sudden change in diet was too much for his body to bear. He died before the trip was over. King Charles arranged for Tom to be buried in Westminster Abby, where his grave can be seen today.

Tom's story illustrates the significant impact of nutrition on health. A healthy diet is the foundation to a long and healthy life. The majority of diseases afflicting our nation today (heart disease, diabetes, obesity, etc.) can be prevented, reversed, or greatly improved by eating a healthy diet. If you want first-class health, you need to eat first-class foods.

First-Class Foods

These foods are powerful tools in your quest for optimal health. They include a variety of whole, plant-based foods, including vegetables, fruits, whole grains, beans, legumes, nuts, and seeds. They are packed with powerful nutrients. For best results, aim for at least 80-90 percent of your calories from first-class foods. Make a giant green salad. Enjoy beans over a baked potato. Replace your usual dessert with a delicious piece of fruit.

Eat a handful of nuts. There are many creative ways to enjoy first-class foods. The healthy recipes in this book will help get you started.

Second-Class Foods

These foods are not nearly as nutrient-dense as first-class foods. They should be used sparingly. Second-class foods include processed whole grains, processed fruits or vegetables (with added sugar, salt, or fat), meat substitutes, organic, fat-free dairy products, free range eggs, and fruit juice.

Third-Class Foods

These foods are at the bottom of the nutritional food chain. They are full of empty calories and proven to promote disease. Third-class foods include refined grains and sweets, meat, cheese and dairy products, processed and packaged foods, deep-fried foods, and fast-foods.

Try to compare your food choices to a stoplight. Imagine that you have a green light for first-class foods, a yellow light for second-class foods, and a red light for third-class foods.

These choices can have a profound influence on your health. First-class eating can take some getting-used to, but you'll be delightfully surprised how delicious it can be.

Exercise

If your doctor prescribed you a new medication that could safely control weight, lower blood pressure, increase energy, enhance mood, increase productivity, strengthen muscles and bones, and decrease the risk for heart disease, stroke, diabetes, Alzheimer's, arthritis, and many other conditions... would you take it? You'd be crazy not to. Although no such pill exists, you can experience all these benefits (and more!) by exercising regularly.

The human body was created to move. Your bones, muscles, joints, and nerves are intricately designed for action. But despite the health benefits of physical activity, only 3.5 percent of Americans between the ages of 18 and 59 get the minimum recommended amount. Forty percent of Americans don't exercise at all. They miss out on the many physical and psychological benefits that active people enjoy.

These benefits are available to you. Regardless of your current fitness level, you can start experiencing the "miracle drug" of exercise today. Let's take a look at three important types of physical activity:

1. Aerobic Exercise:
Get that Heart Beating!

Aim for 30-45 minutes of aerobic exercise, at least 5 times per week. You can build up to this gradually. Try walking, jogging, biking, swimming, cycling, etc... Find something you enjoy and someone to enjoy it with. Aerobic exercise will improve your circulation, boost your metabolism, enhance your mood, and decrease your risk for many diseases.

2. After-Meal Exercise:
Get those Legs Moving!

A short walk after each meal is a great way to optimize digestion and clear your mind. If you struggle with prediabetes or diabetes, this habit will also help prevent blood-sugar spikes. Even a five or ten minute walk can make a difference. After-meal exercise should be less intense than aerobic exercise.

3. Strength Training:
Work those Muscles!

Once you're comfortable with aerobic and after-meal exercise, you may want to add strength (resistance) training to your routine. You can use weights, bands, or other forms of resistance. This training should strengthen your major muscle groups, boost your metabolism, and prevent future mobility problems. Aim for 20 minutes of strength training, two to three times per week. Start with just a few minutes, then build up gradually. Choose safe equipment and learn to use it properly.

Don't be afraid to start out small! Make a plan. Find a buddy. Be consistent. Chances are, once you start enjoying the benefits of exercise, you won't want to stop!

Water

How much water will you use today? Between showering, flushing the toilet, brushing teeth, washing dishes, and doing laundry and other tasks, most Americans use about 100 gallons each day. Despite this unrestrained (and often wasteful) use, many Americans suffer from chronic, mild dehydration.

The human body is composed of 60 percent water. Every cell, tissue, organ, and system needs sufficient water to survive and thrive. Adequate hydration cleanses the body, improves circulation, boosts immunity, improves mental functioning, lowers inflammation, optimizes digestion, and provides countless other health benefits.

Dehydration has both short and long-term negative effects. Short-term symptoms include fatigue, sluggishness, irritability, headaches, constipation, overeating, dry skin and lips, and decreased mental performance. Long-term effects include premature aging, stress on joints and organs, kidney damage, toxin buildup, increased risk for injury and infection, weight gain, and increased risk for heart attack and stroke.

If you're fortunate enough to have access to clean water, you don't have to suffer these effects. Drinking adequate water is one of the most simple, affordable, and powerful health strategies you can follow.

How Much to Drink

Most adults need eight to ten cups of water per day. This amount varies depending on body size, activity level, and environment. One rule of thumb is to drink half an ounce of water for every pound of body weight. For example, a person weighing 150 pounds would drink 75 ounces (about 9 cups) of water each day. Another way to monitor your hydration level is to pay attention to the color of your urine. Clear or slightly yellow urine indicates adequate hydration, while dark urine suggests dehydration.

When to Drink

The best times to drink water are 1) When you wake up, and 2) Between Meals. The body is most dehydrated in the morning. Drinking one to two cups of water when you first wake up is the first step to a well-hydrated day. The next step is to stay well hydrated between meals. Drink one to two cups of water mid-morning and mid-afternoon. Drinking water between meals instead of with meals can improve digestion. However, if you are already dehydrated at mealtime, go ahead and drink. The amount of water you drink is more important than the time at which you drink it.

Why not start today? There's no better time to experience the life-giving benefits of H_2O.

Sunshine

Ninety-three million miles from earth is a giant, fiery ball of flaming hot plasma- the sun. This 10,000°F star is the center of our solar system in more ways than one. Not only do eight planets revolve around it, but the sun accounts for 99.8 percent of the mass of the solar system. It would take 1.3 million earths to fit inside the sun. This massive star provides us with multiple health benefits. Regular sun exposure enhances mood, reduces stress, alleviates pain, synchronizes hormones, and improves sleep and digestion.

But that's just the beginning! Sun exposure stimulates the body's production of Vitamin D, a hormone that impacts nearly every aspect of health. People with adequate levels of Vitamin D are less likely to suffer from a variety of diseases.

Vitamin D Helps Prevent[1]:

- ▶ Diabetes
- ▶ Cancer
- ▶ Heart disease
- ▶ Obesity
- ▶ Colds, flus, and other common illnesses
- ▶ Infections
- ▶ Autoimmune Disorders
- ▶ Mental Illness

Unfortunately, the vast majority of Americans are Vitamin D deficient. One of the most simple and effective strategies you can follow to improve your health is to optimize your Vitamin D level. Ask your doctor to order the 25 Hydroxy Vitamin D test to evaluate your level. Standard lab guidelines state that any level between 30 and 100 ng/mL is adequate. However, many Vitamin D experts agree that the higher end of this range is much healthier. A level of 30 ng/mL may prevent osteoporosis and rickets, but higher levels are needed to help prevent other diseases. A better goal is to aim for a blood level of 50-100 ng/mL.

Although sun exposure does produce Vitamin D, many people find that they need supplementation to keep their levels high enough. If you're deficient, you can take 10,000 units of Vitamin D per day for several months, then check your blood levels again. Once your ranges are optimal, you can usually maintain them with 6,000 units per day (for men) and 5,000 units per day (for women). Vitamin D toxicity is very rare, and does not occur until the blood level is over 200. Continue to check your level every fall and spring, as levels fluctuate depending on the season.

To enjoy sunlight's many other health benefits, aim for 20-30 minutes of direct sun exposure, at least three or four times per week. Follow the advice of wise King Solomon who said: "Truly the light is sweet, and it is pleasant for the eyes to behold the sun.[2]"

1. Vitamin D Council (2013)
2. Ecclesiastes 11:7 (NKJV)

Balance

The dictionary defines balance as: "a condition in which different elements are equal or in the correct proportions." Balance is important for everyone, but especially for tightrope walkers. In 2012, a Chinese acrobat fell 650 feet into a gorge while walking backwards, blindfolded, on a 2,300 foot rope. Miraculously, the sixth-generation tightrope walker survived.

Chances are, you've never walked a tightrope. But everyday life is a balancing act of its own. Work. Family. Finances. Friends. Health. Plans. As you juggle multiple priorities and deadlines, it becomes increasingly challenging to live a balanced life. However, balance is possible. With God's help, you can prioritize your choices to experience optimal health. Here are a few strategies to help:

1. Prioritize Your Health

Your health influences every other aspect of life. Take time to invest in your physical, emotional, and spiritual well-being. This will improve your overall productivity and effectiveness. Eat first-class foods. Exercise regularly. Drink adequate water. Get sunlight. Breathe fresh air. Get adequate sleep. Spend quality time with family and friends. Set aside quiet time for prayer, Bible study and reflection. These simple habits will work wonders to improve your health and enhance your quality of life.

2. Avoid Harmful Things

Allow your new, healthy choices to replace unhealthy choices of the past. Some habits just don't belong in a healthy lifestyle. The use of drugs and alcohol should be completely avoided. These substances impair judgment, paving the way for more unhealthy choices. Alcohol causes almost 4 percent of deaths worldwide, more than AIDS, tuberculosis, or violence.[1] Smoking and tobacco should also be avoided. Each year, over 400,000 Americans die prematurely from smoking or exposure to second-hand smoke.[2] Caffeinated beverages promote fatigue and premature aging. Some foods are better left uneaten. Some forms of entertainment are better left untouched. Ask God to show you which habits are causing you harm. He can give you power to replace them with good habits.

3. Carefully Use Helpful Things

Healthy choices are most healthy when made in the right proportions. It's easy to focus on one or two aspects of health, while ignoring the others. Health is a comprehensive, dynamic process. True wellness comes from carefully balancing a variety of healthy choices.

"Beloved, I pray that you may prosper in all things and be in health, just as your soul prospers." —3 John 1:2 (NKJV)

1. WHO(2011)
2. CDC (2012)

Fresh Air

In the past 24 hours, your heart beat 100,000 times, your eyelids blinked 9,000 times, and you swallowed 1,500 times. All this occurred without conscious effort on your part.

Breath is another function of the body that comes automatically. Unless you suffer from respiratory distress, you likely don't give much thought to breathing. But breathing keeps you alive on a minute-to-minute basis. You can live weeks without food and days without water, but only minutes without oxygen.

You breathe about 20,000 times per day. As you inhale, oxygen travels to your lungs and then passes into your bloodstream. This oxygen is vitally important for your brain and every cell in your body. As you exhale, toxic carbon dioxide exits your body. Each day, you breathe in over 2,000 gallons of air.

Although God designed breathing to be innate, there are several ways to make sure you get the maximum benefit from each breath.

1. Get Fresh Air

The best air to breathe is fresh, outdoor air, found in places with low levels of pollution. Believe it or not, this air is chemically different than stagnant, indoor air. The negatively charged ions found in fresh air provide a variety of health benefits, including improved mood and mental functioning, increased oxygen in the blood, decreased anxiety, improved digestion, and decreased risk of infection.[1]

The negative ions in fresh air are destroyed with pollution or recirculation of indoor air (breathing the same air repeatedly). Indoor air can be up to five times more polluted than outdoor air.[2] Polluted air contributes to headaches, irritability, fatigue, and increased risk of infection and disease.

To improve your air quality, enjoy fresh, outdoor air and regularly ventilate indoor rooms with outdoor air. Just keeping the windows open from time to time can make a big difference. If you live in a polluted area, air your home out at night when smog levels are decreased. Be sure to change air filters regularly. You may want to invest in an air-purifier for your home.

2. Breathe Deeply

To fully benefit from oxygen exchange, you need to breathe deeply. Shallow breathing causes anxiety and tension. Practice deep breathing by placing a hand over your abdomen. Take long, slow breaths, filling your lungs to capacity. Your hand should rise with your abdomen. Deep breathing promotes relaxation and enhanced oxygen exchange. Take a deep breath, and see for yourself!

1. Nedley, Neil. Proof Positive. (1999)
2. Amazing Health Facts Magazine (2009)

Rest

The Koala is the sleepiest creature in the animal kingdom. It sleeps away 22 hours of every day. The sloth comes in at a close second, snoozing for 20 hours. Armadillos and opossums tie for third place, with 19 hours each.

Fortunately, humans don't need as much sleep as these creatures. If we did, it would be hard to accomplish anything else. **If you're an adult, you need between 7 and 8 hours of sleep per night.** If you're like two-thirds of Americans, you don't get that much. You may feel you have "too much to do" to sleep. But sleep deprivation significantly decreases productivity. It also lowers your immune system, increases your risk for many diseases, decreases your mental functioning, and last (but not least) makes you feel like a sloth.

There are five key strategies you can follow to get the maximum benefit from sleep. These simple solutions will refresh your body and recharge your mind:

1. Set the Right Bedtime.

There's no better way to make sleep a priority. Plan ahead to get 7 to 8 hours of sleep each night. The hours of sleep before midnight are more valuable than the later hours, so set your bedtime early. Ben Franklin was spot on when he said: "Early to bed and early to rise makes a man healthy, wealthy, and wise."

2. Get Regular Exercise

Being active early in the day will help you fall asleep and stay asleep. For best results, exercise in the morning or early afternoon. If you wait until evening, exercise will wake you up instead of winding you down.

3. Don't Eat Late

A large meal in the evening interferes with sleep. Try to make supper the smallest meal of your day, and eat it several hours before bedtime.

4. Optimize Your Environment

Your sleeping environment should be dark, slightly cool, and quiet. A dark room boosts your body's melatonin production. Slightly cool air induces sleepiness. A quiet room minimizes distractions.

5. Relax Before Bedtime

Put away your work. Dim the lights. Do something to unwind. Avoid watching TV or working on your computer or phone. Backlit devices make it more difficult to fall asleep.

You can also improve your sleep by getting sunlight in the morning, avoiding naps late in the day, and staying away from caffeine and other stimulants.

Put these tips to the test! You will find that improving your sleep will also enhance every other area of your life.

Trust in God

The world is full of broken promises. Advertisements promise miraculous results from nearly every product imaginable. Potato chips will make you popular. Magical cream will melt away pounds. The right shampoo will solve your relationship woes. You've learned that if it sounds too good to be true, it probably is. Regardless of inflated promises, stuff will always let you down.

People also let you down. Over fifty percent of marriages end in divorce. An act of child abuse is reported every ten seconds. Acts of domestic violence and terrorism are at an all-time high.

In a world of broken promises and broken people, is there anyone left to trust? Many people find hope and comfort in the realization that there is one being in the universe who is completely trustworthy- God. Faith in God provides a variety of emotional, mental, and even physical health benefits.

Faith and Health

Evidence from over 1,200 studies and 400 reviews reveals a strong correlation between faith and health.[1] One study that followed over 21,000 people found that those who regularly attended religious services lived an average of seven years longer than those who did not.[2] Prayer has also been linked to a variety of health benefits, including better surgery outcomes, decreased headaches, lower blood pressure, decreased inflammation, and decreased risk of chronic disease.

Spirituality also influences mental health. Religious involvement is correlated with higher self-esteem, less depression and anxiety, greater social support, lower rates of suicide, lower rates of alcohol and drug abuse, less criminal activity, and greater marital satisfaction.

You can experience the healing benefits of faith by following these simple steps.

1. Connect with God

You have a compassionate Creator who longs to guide and bless your journey through life. His love is unconditional. You can connect with Him through prayer and by reading His Word- The Bible. Don't be afraid to start out small. The more time you spend in communication with God, the more you will be drawn to Him. "Taste and see that the Lord is good; blessed is the man who trusts in Him.[3]"

2. Connect with Others

Connecting with other believers is essential for spiritual health. Find a supportive faith community whose beliefs are grounded in God's Word. Surround yourself with people who will encourage you on your journey toward health and wholeness.

1. Christian Medical Fellowship (2011)
2. Hummer, Robert, et al. (1999)
3. Psalm 34:8 (NKJV)

Blue Zones

Longevity Secrets from the Longest-Living People on Earth

How much would you pay to live an extra decade? Increased longevity isn't for sale, but it is available. How? We find the answer in a riveting *National Geographic* article called *The Secrets of Living Longer.*[1] It describes three different "Blue Zones," locations that are home to the longest-living people on earth. These are: Okinawa, Japan, Sardinia, Italy, and Loma Linda, California. The Blue Zones share several key longevity secrets:[2]

► Moderate physical activity built into everyday life

► Healthy ways to relax and relieve stress

► A clear sense of purpose and meaning

► A plant-based diet which includes beans

► Maintaining a healthy weight

► Strong faith and participation in faith-based services

► Close family relationships

► Supportive social networks

Each Blue Zone stays healthy in its own unique way. A typical morning in the life of an elderly Sardinian man might include milking cows, chopping wood, and walking five miles with his sheep. Later in the day, he will join his wife, children, grandchildren, great-grandchildren, and great-great grandchildren for a delicious, plant-based meal.

Before mealtime in Okinawa, family members recite the ancient Confucian adage: Hara Hachi Bunme, translated as, "Eat until you are eight parts (out of ten) full." This clever saying prevents overeating. Okinawans also have a solution for social isolation. They form what is called the moai, close-knit support groups built of friends that stay together for life. To maintain a clear sense of purpose and meaning, Okinawan's are taught to have a personal ikigai, that is, "a reason to get up in the morning."

Seventh-day Adventists reduce stress by taking a twenty-four hour Sabbath rest each week. From sunset Friday night to sunset Saturday, they lay aside the responsibilities and pressures of the week to focus exclusively on God, family, nature, and community. Many Seventh-day Adventists are vegetarian. These habits help explain why Adventists in the United States live about a decade longer than the average American.[3]

You don't have to live in a Blue Zone, milk a cow, or recite a Confucian adage to increase your longevity. The good news is, you can follow the Blue Zone secrets in your own unique way to live a longer, healthier, and happier life. Why not start today?

1. Buettner, Dan. *The Secrets of Living Longer.* National Geographic, November 2005.
2. Buettner, Dan. "How to live to be 100+" www.ted.com
3. Adventist Health Study. (1976-2002)

Benefits of an Adventist Lifestyle

Let's take a closer look at one of the world's longest-living people groups—Seventh-day Adventists. Loma Linda, California was featured as a Blue Zone in the *National Geographic* article *Secrets to Living Longer*, because it has a concentrated population of long-living Seventh-day Adventists. However, many Adventists throughout the United States and worldwide also enjoy a longevity edge. In fact, Seventh-day Adventists in the United States live about a decade longer than other Americans. A recent *U.S News and World Report* article entitled *Eleven Health Habits that Will Help You Live to 100*, listed habit # 8 as: "Live like a Seventh-day Adventist."

In addition to a longer lifespan, Adventists also enjoy lower risk of disease, including heart disease, diabetes, several cancers, high blood pressure, and arthritis.

The Adventist Blue Zone can't be explained by genetics or geography. Seventh-day Adventists are a diverse group of people. Some are born into Adventist families. Others join the faith later in life. Adventists come from a wide range of cultural, ethnic, and socioeconomic backgrounds.

What's The Secret?

If genes and geography can't explain the Adventist longevity edge, what can? The answer is lifestyle. Adventists from all walks of life are encouraged to follow Biblical principles of health and spirituality. What are those principles? The same strategies outlined in this book: a healthy, plant-based diet, regular exercise, water, sunshine, balance, the avoidance of unhealthy substances, fresh air, physical and spiritual rest, social support, and trust in God.

Because Adventist longevity is based on healthy habits rather than genetics or environment, it has the potential to survive unhealthy cultural changes. Unfortunately, other Blue Zones are starting to experience a decrease in longevity as the western diet creeps into their backyards. Seventh-day Adventists aren't immune to these health risks, but those who choose to follow the healthy habits they've been taught will continue to experience countless benefits.

You're Invited

If you'd like to learn more about Seventh-day Adventists or are looking for a supportive community of faith in which to grow, you are always welcome to visit a Seventh-day Adventist church. Seventh-day Adventists believe that God's message of love and healing is designed for every member of humanity- including you. We'd love to help support you in your journey toward optimal health. For more information, visit www.adventist.org

1. Buettner, Dan. *The Secrets of Living Longer.* National Geographic, November 2005.
2. Adventist Health Study. (1976-2002)
3. Adventist Health Study. (1976-2002)

Product Info

Vegan Gourmet Cream Cheese Made by Follow Your Heart this non-dairy cream cheese is made with 76% organic ingredients. It works well in any recipe that calls for cream cheese.

Vegan Gourmet Sour Cream Made by Follow Your Heart this non-dairy sour cream is made with 70% organic ingredients and is a perfect replacement in any recipe that uses sour cream.

Bragg's Liquid Aminos This is a liquid soy protein that seasons food. It's lower in sodium than soy sauce. Found in a health food store. Can be used in place of soy sauce.

Desserts You will notice I have a section for desserts in this book. We try to limit our desserts to once a week. I usually make a fruit pie of some type. Most of the desserts have about 3 gm of fiber per serving, so at least you are getting some fiber in it. Try to keep your desserts to a minimum, and when you do make them, enjoy to the max!

Silver Hills High Fiber Bread Silver Hills Bakery makes delicious breads. Their breads are made with sprouted grains which gives a major boost to the nutrient content and they are high in fiber, the Mack's Flax and Squirrelly bread have 5 grams of fiber per slice. Check out the variety of other wonderful breads at www.silverhillsbakery.com

VeganEgg Made by Follow Your Heart. These "eggs" are cholesterol free and 100% plant based. They work great in recipes that call for eggs, or you can scramble them too.

Honey You will notice that I have used honey in some of my recipes. If you prefer not to use honey, substitute with pure maple syrup.

Instant Food Thickener A corn starch thickener that can be added to foods without cooking the food. Made by Diamond Crystal. Phone number 800-227-4455.

Margarine If you use margarine, Earth Balance is a brand that is non-hydrogenated and has good flavor. Read the label on Smart Balance, some of their varieties have whey in them, which is a milk product.

Misto Sprayer An air pump olive oil sprayer that can be ordered on the Internet.

Non-Dairy Whipped Topping You can make your own in a pinch. Use 2 cans of full fat coconut milk. Refrigerate for at least a day. When you're ready to make the whipped topping, put a glass bowl in the refrigerator for 10 minutes, then take your cold bowl, and can's of coconut milk. Open the cans and remove just the white solid coconut from the can and leave the remaining liquid in the can. Put the solid coconut milk in the bowl and whip with an electric mixer adding 2-3 Tbs organic powdered sugar as you whip. Beat the coconut milk until it forms a nice whipped topping. Works perfectly on any dish and tastes great!

Olive Oil Extra virgin olive oil is the oil of choice. It's loaded with antioxidants and is the only oil I use. I use the extra virgin oil for salad dressings and to sauté foods. I use the extra light olive oil

for baking, because I don't want the olive taste in some foods. Studies have shown that olive oil actually helps with memory by binding with toxins that promote Alzheimer's disease.[1]

1. *Toxicology and Applied Pharmacology*, volume 240, Issue 2, Oct. 2009.

Dairy Free Cheese There are several brands to choose from. For sliced cheese we like the Provolone Slices by Follow Your Heart for making sandwiches. Another brand that's a favorite is Chao cheese slices, the original flavor made by Field Roast. For shredded cheeses we like Daiya brand cheese or Nut Cheese made with cashew milk made by Parmela Creamery. Shop around and see which one you like best!

Rumford Baking Powder This baking powder doesn't have any aluminum in it. You want to avoid aluminum, as it contributes to Alzheimer's disease.

Soymilk I prefer to use the unsweetened soymilk. It has very few ingredients in it and cuts down on calories, as well.

Stevia This is an herb often called "sweet leaf." It usually comes in powder form, and only a small amount is needed to sweeten your food. Stevia is essentially calorie free, and the body processes it slowly, so it doesn't cause a spike in blood sugar. It doesn't work for every recipe, but when it can be used, it's a great natural sweetener.

Tortilla Wraps La Tortilla brand wraps are wonderful. They are loaded with fiber—12 - 13 gms in each wrap. When making your veggie wraps, look for this brand. Most health food stores carry them, and even some grocery stores have them.

Vegenaise A tasty, non-dairy mayonaise that's found in the refrigerator section of a health food store. It has no cholesterol.

Vegetarian Chicken or Beef Seasoning There are three brands to choose from— McKay's, Bill's Best, or Vegetarian Express. Most health food stores have McKay's seasonings, although some of their seasonings have milk or whey in them. You would have to ask to order the vegan variety.

Vital Wheat Gluten Also known as Do-Pep, this is a high-gluten flour used to make gluten steaks or added to bread to give it a nice consistency.

Vegex or Savorex Yeast extract used as a flavor enhancer. It can be found in health food stores.

Yeast The best yeast I've found for bread making is Saf-Instant. It comes in a 16-oz size and lasts a long time. Once I open it, I freeze it and just use it as needed. You can usually find this in a health food store.

THE FOLLOWING TRADEMARKED™ AND / OR REGISTERED® PRODUCT BRAND NAMES ARE USED IN THIS BOOK: Pam cooking spray, McKay's chicken style seasoning, Bill's Best, Rumford baking powder, Vitamix, Blendtec, Morningstar Farms products, Lawry's, Mrs. Dash, Vegenaise, Better Than Sour Cream, Better Than Cream Cheese, Bubbie's pickles, Frontier Mexican seasoning, Tony's seasoning, Campbell's Healthy Request soups, Spike seasoning, Pepperidge Farm, Worthington FriChik, La Tortilla, Do-Pep, Vegex, Savorex, Cedar Lake, Ener-G Foods, Tofutti, Barilla, Bragg's Liquid Aminos, Earth Balance margarine, Silk soymilk, Roma, Pero, Mori-nu Mates pudding mixes, Soyatoo, Diamond Crystal, Mimic Cream, Oroweat Double Fiber, Truwhip, Parma Zaan Sprinkles, Saf-Instant, and Misto

Gift Baskets

Extending yourself to someone by taking them a home-made gift can strengthen friendships, or even make new friends. Through the years, I have taken a loaf of home-made bread to new neighbors who have moved into the area. The response has always been very positive. On one occasion, the neighbors had just moved here and didn't know anyone. Dan and I walked over and knocked on their door. The lady opened the door and saw me standing there with the loaf of bread in my hands, and she threw her arms open and welcomed me with a hug! We became fast friends and now are even best of friends.

Get Well Basket

When you know of someone who has become ill—particularly someone who lives alone and has no one to look after them—a basket filled with health-promoting foods is a welcome sight. You can fill the basket with fresh fruit, home-made bread, nuts, fruit juice, etc.

Banana Bread

If you want to take a loaf of banana bread to your neighbor, you can make it look really special in the way you present it. At various craft stores you can find boxes and fancy lace paper or tissue paper—and then adding a fresh flower or two makes it even more appealing.

Simple Gifts

Sometimes you just want to let someone know you are thinking of them. A simple home-made gift of granola, date bars, fresh nuts, a little pie, or whatever it is you make that day can brighten up someone else's life. I always keep some small pie plates on hand, so that when I'm making a pie for our family I can make a little extra for someone else.

Christmas Basket

A Christmas basket is fun to do. When making a basket for a family, I usually like to make a large pot of soup. I try to label the items in the basket so people can know what they're getting. Of course, with the soup goes a loaf of home-made bread. I put the bread in a plastic bag and then tie raffia around it and put in some sprigs of wheat on the top. Sometimes I will put a label or a gift tag on the bread.

A small box of crackers goes well with soup. Then add a bottle of sparkling juice. And hanging a Christmas tree ornament over it makes it more festive. I load the basket with fresh fruit and slip a kitchen towel through the handle of the basket. A small green plant adds color—or a little flowering plant. I usually include a dessert, and you can even put a serving plate to go with it. This basket is filled with a meal they can enjoy and is packed with love from you.

Food is something everyone can enjoy, and home-made food is even better. God bless you as you share with others and are a blessing to them.

Gardening

Growing a garden and having fruit trees is a major blessing. It doesn't matter if you have a small yard or not, you can still plant a tree somewhere. My husband thinks that my goal is to cover every inch of our property with fruit trees! Well, he's close to right! There's nothing like growing your own fruits and vegetables. You know what you're getting. You don't have to deal with pesticides or chemicals.

If you live in a city or apartment and don't have the ability to grow trees or plant a garden, you can have an herb garden in your house or sprout some seeds to add to your salads and sandwiches. You can grow something, wherever you live.

Not only do you benefit from your fruit being free of chemicals, you are outdoors in the sunlight, breathing fresh air and soaking up some Vitamin D from the sun. If you worry that bending down will cause those aches and pains, make a box garden, or you can buy them ready made. You will enjoy watching the plants grow or the seeds sprout, and seeing the fruit grow on the trees reminds you of our Creator and how He has bountifully blessed us.

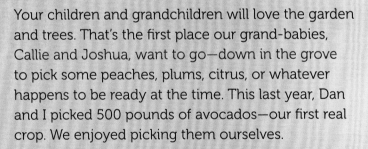

Your children and grandchildren will love the garden and trees. That's the first place our grand-babies, Callie and Joshua, want to go—down in the grove to pick some peaches, plums, citrus, or whatever happens to be ready at the time. This last year, Dan and I picked 500 pounds of avocados—our first real crop. We enjoyed picking them ourselves.

You can take some of your fruit, if you have an abundance, and dehydrate it, or we freeze the peaches and apples. I freeze my apples in 6 C measurements so that if I want to make a pie, they are all sliced and ready to go. Sharing with friends is fun too.

Whatever you do, if you plant something, enjoy it to the max. God has promised to bless "the fruit of your land"—Deuteronomy 7:13.

Thank You's

It seems there are so many people to thank, and I want to thank them all, but there are a few who have really helped make the cookbook special and the cooking show flow smoothly.

I first want to thank **Brad & Kandus Thorpe** for the invitation to do the Naturally Gourmet™ cooking show for the Hope Channel. Thanks for the vote of confidence and allowing me to expand my ministry.

My right arm of this cookbook and cooking show was **Donna Hanson**—helping to set up for the show, set up and arrange food for the photography, etc. Couldn't have done it without Donna! Thanks for your hours of work, dedication, and friendship.

Thanks to **Joy Sajdak**, who came from Wisconsin to help with the cooking show. She steadily worked away at setting up, cleaning up, helping with the food, etc. What a friend! Thanks, Joy!

Lavon Metzker cooked up a storm for each show!

Donna Hanson helped make things beautiful every day.

The heavy duty work of preparing food and ingredients for food demos for the show was done by **Lavon Metzker**—outstanding job done. Thank you so much Lavon.

Use of a beautiful kitchen with 10-foot ceilings was provided by **Debbie & Mac McClanahan**—thank you so much for sharing!

For his expertise, knowledge, and clear explanations of complex nutritional information, I want to thank **Dr. Wes Youngberg.** What a blessing he was to the show.

For their willingness to help and assist in any way, I want to thank both of my daughters in law—**Erin** and **Sondra Houghton**. You did a great job!

For excellent photography for this cookbook, I'm grateful for **Elena Gipson** and my husband, **Dan Houghton**.

For cookbook design, my hat's off to **Mark Bond**. Couldn't have done a better job. Mark was as excited about this book as I have been. That's what it takes! You're the best!

The behind-the-scenes person no one knows about, yet who has spent hours on the computer analyzing every recipe, is my friend and dietitian, **Eileen Kuninobu**. What a blessing you have been! Thank you so much!

My son Jamey did the demo for bread making.

And last but not least, I want to thank my husband **Dan** for his support in this ministry. He has always been behind me and cheering me on. And to our sons, **Danny** and **Jamey**, I'm thankful you were such good taste testers as I've experimented with new recipes. To sum it up, it takes a lot of people to make it all work, and I'm just one thankful person for all the people God has put in my life.

Through the 15-plus years that I have been teaching vegetarian cooking classes, I have had a loyal friend at my side helping me with cooking, chopping, setting up, etc.—and that is **Dorthy Grey**. I will always be grateful to **Dorthy** for all her help and encouragement.

Many other friends and family members have helped in this ministry, and I can't name them all, but I will list the names of some who have really been a blessing in one way or another. They include: **Sue Knutson, Margo Meese, Bennie Phillips, Joe & Andrea Atchison, Donna Hanson, Jodi Bencomo, Selina Preciado, Telecia Cooke, Joi Cooke, Yvonne Dawkins, Don & Kay Rozelle, Debbie Foll, Tammy Hayton, Gene, Jean & Bruce Hildebrand, Betsy Phillips, Teenie Finley, Nema Johnson, Nathaly Krkljus, Andrew and Eileen Kuninobu, Melinda Liou, Sam Liou, Bonnie Molitor, Marivi Musgrave, Donna Ferguson, Wendy Nelson, Linda Zinke, Ed & Joy Sajdak, Sonja Nicola, Betty Tiffany, Harold & Judy Van Dyke, Barb Flees, Shirlee Kehney, Inez Torres, Kathy Uraine, Sandy Williams, Shashi Lopez, Linda Kennedy** and **Silvana Sorace**. Any names I've missed, I apologize—each person was a blessing.

My son Danny did one show with me, pictured here with Wes Youngberg.

Family and friends came on this day. Dorthy and Heidy joined us.

Recommended Resources

Twenty Four Realistic Ways to Improve Your Health by Dr. Tim Arnott. This is an awesome little book that's packed with valuable information on simple ways you can stay healthy. I can't recommend this book enough to you.

Depression, the Way Out by Dr. Neil Nedley. If you or someone you know suffers from depression, this book is an excellent resource. It shows how you can overcome depression the natural way.

The Best of Silver Hills Cookbook by Eileen Brewer. I've used recipes from this cookbook in my cooking classes. They are great recipes and good for you too. Eileen has a new cookbook out called *Silver Hills Spa Cuisine*.

The Total Vegetarian by Barbara Watson. Another cookbook I've used in my classes that has tasty, health-promoting recipes.

The Vegetarian Express This company provides seasonings such as the Parma Zaan cheese—a substitute for parmesan cheese. They carry a ranch seasoning that you just add to Vegenaise for a salad dressing. You can order by phone and have it shipped to you, or some health food stores carry their products. Phone number: 734-355-3593.

Natural Lifestyle Cooking Ernestine "Teenie" Finley has conducted hundreds of cooking schools over the years. This book is the accumulation of many of the recipes that have been taste-tested in these schools and in the Finley family kitchen. With a hard cover spiral binding and full-color pictures throughout, this cookbook is not only attractive, but very user-friendly.

Naturally Gourmet™
Cooking Series on DVD

If you like this cookbook, you'll love cooking along with host, **Karen Houghton** on the popular series featured on the **Hope Channel**. This DVD set contains 14 shows with 7 hours of heart-healthy programming!

Dr. Wes Youngberg co-hosts each episode. He brings a wealth of information with healthy facts from the latest medical studies.

To order your copy, visit www.NaturallyGourmet.com!

Bread of Life

It is written, "Man shall not live by bread alone, but by every word that proceeds out of the mouth of God." — Matthew 4:4

1 part prayer

1 part Bible study

1 pinch faith

1 dash hope

1 bucket full of love

Generous helping of fellowship

Heaping Tbs of forgiveness

We thought it would be good to include just one more bonus recipe that we've found to be amazing in our lives. Mix all the ingredients and let them rise each morning. Don't be discouraged if it doesn't turn out perfectly the first day. It takes a lifetime of practice to master, but it's worth the effort. This recipe is one that we try to bake every single day. It's best served with the fruit of the Spirit. (Love, joy peace, patience, kindness, goodness, faithfulness, gentleness, and self control.)

(Hint: A sweet spirit also makes it turn out better!)

Nutrition Facts

Calories 0, Fat 0 g, Saturated 0 g, Polyunsaturated 0 g, Monounsaturated 0 g, Trans fat 0 g, Cholesterol 0 mg, Sodium 0 mg, Carbohydrate 0 g, Dietary fiber 0 g, Protein 0 g, Vitamin A 0%, Vitamin C 0%, Calcium 0%, Iron 0%

Recommended Resources

If you're serious about making the "Bread of Life" a part of your daily routine, here are some great resources to get you started from our friends at **It Is Written:**

It Is Written Bible Study Guides

The *It Is Written* Bible Study Guides are a great way to learn the timeless truths of God's Word. These 25 guides are attractive, modern, and easy to use.

- Simple Q&A format, with the answer key included.
- High-quality photos and artwork.
- Twenty-five lessons covering all the major Bible themes.
- Each lesson stands on its own.

itiswritten.com/biblestudy
https://itiswritten.shop/iiw-bible-study-guide-set-1-25.html

Watch It Is Written

In our flagship television series, *It Is Written,* host John Bradshaw takes you on a journey through Scripture each week. You will learn key truths of the Bible and gain a deeper understanding of God. *It Is Written* consistently ranks as one of the top 10 religious television programs in the United States. The program's reach extends to more than 140 countries and regularly airs on multiple channels. Watch *It Is Written* online at itiswritten.com/television

Download the It Is Written App

Watch *It Is Written* on the go. Download the It Is Written app. Access Every Word™— short daily devotional by Pastor John Bradshaw, blog posts, weekly programs, submit prayer requests, and more with ease. To download the It Is Written app on your mobile device search for "It Is Written" in the App Store℠ or on Google Play™.

App Store is a service mark of Apple Inc. Google Play is a trademark of Google Inc.